VICTORIANS ALL

VICTORIANS ALL

BY

FLORA MASSON

KENNIKAT PRESS
Port Washington, N. Y./London

VICTORIANS ALL
First published in 1931
Reissued in 1970 by Kennikat Press
Library of Congress Catalog Card No: 75-105806
ISBN 0-8046-0962-4

Manufactured by Taylor Publishing Company   Dallas, Texas

CONTENTS

ACKNOWLEDGMENT

SOME of the material of this volume has been published in the *Scotsman,* the *Cornhill Magazine,* and the *University of Edinburgh Journal,* and is now reprinted with the kind permission of the Editors.

Use has also been made of an article which appeared in the *Pall Mall Magazine,* now no longer existing.

The Recollections of R. L. S. are reproduced from *I Can Remember Robert Louis Stevenson,* by permission of the Editor.

FLORA MASSON.

VICTORIANS ALL

CHAPTER I

MAINLY ABOUT DICKENS AND THACKERAY

I can remember my father, David Masson, sitting at a writing-table in his study, writing with a quill pen that sometimes made a scratching noise. A rifle stood in one corner of the room; a sword was slung against the wall; books were piled on the floor; and sometimes—but that was a very serious occupation—he was cleaning his rifle, and we could investigate a fascinating coat that hung over a chair—a coat of soft dust-grey, with indigo blue at the collar and wrists: a coat adorned with the silver buttons of the London Scottish of that day.

My father was then a man nearing forty, and it was a good many years since he had come to London, at four-and-twenty, resolved to make a living by his pen. Friends he had made, almost at once: Carlyle and his wife, in Chelsea; John Stuart Mill and the Mill family, in Kensington Square; Mazzini, the patriot-refugee, with the Stansfelds and

7

others of a political circle working, inside and outside of Parliament, for the Freedom and Unity of Italy. The "Society of the Friends of Italy" had made him its first secretary. Literary work also he had found, especially on the staff of the *Athenæum*, under the editorship of T. K. Hervey; and he was writing for W. & R. Chambers's Educational Series, and for the *North British Review*.

At that time the very able and energetic young editor of the *North British Review* was Alexander Campbell Fraser. He and my father had been college friends in Edinburgh, —they were afterwards to be colleagues on the Senatus of Edinburgh University. What more natural than that they should be helping each other, and that when *Pendennis* and *David Copperfield* came out, the two novels of the moment, Campbell Fraser should write from Edinburgh, asking his friend for an article on the two works, and incidentally on the two novelists? He stipulated that, if possible, the article should not exceed thirty-two pages; and he added the words of brotherly encouragement, "I anticipate a *chef-d'œuvre*."

It was a happy editorial thought that a copy of the *Review* containing the article should be sent "with the Author's compliments" to Dickens and to Thackeray.

"Your paper," wrote the young editor in the letter which carried this suggestion, "is much applauded." And so the copies were sent, and acknowledgments were duly received—Dickens's letter to be remembered only as "very pleasant, but there was nothing particular about it." Thackeray's letter to be cherished always, not only for its own sake, but because in it he spoke so enthusiastically of Dickens.

It is sometimes of interest to find out what a man was doing and feeling at the time when he wrote some letter, by which in after years he was to be judged or criticised. Dickens's little note—he was "truly gratified by the praise which is so eloquently and thoughtfully bestowed"—was dated from his house in Devonshire Terrace, "Ninth May 1851"; and it was written on paper with a mourning edge. He had, in fact, returned to London from the death-bed of his father, in time to preside and make his great speech at the Theatrical Fund Dinner on April 14th; and on that same night, after his speech, he had been told—I think by his sister-in-law, Miss Hogarth—as he came up the doorsteps of his house in Devonshire Terrace, of the death of his baby-daughter, "Dora Annie," eight months old. When Dickens wrote the polite

little note to his unknown reviewer, the baby
had been dead nearly four weeks.   Dickens
was occupied with the preparations for the
performance of the farce by himself and
Mark Lemon, *Mr. Nightingale's Diary*, which,
with Lytton's comedy *Not so Bad as We
Seem*, was to be played on May 27th at the
Duke of Devonshire's house in Piccadilly,
before the Queen and the Prince Consort.

With Thackeray it was different.   For
him there were no theatricals in view, though
he too was a busy man, and overwrought.
His *Pendennis*, as we know, had been delayed
by a severe illness, and it was dedicated to
the good doctor who "would take no other
fee but thanks."   In May 1851 Thackeray
was preparing his course of lectures on the
English Humourists, the first of which was to
be delivered at Willis's Rooms, on May 22nd.

Willis's Rooms and the *English Humourists*
on the 22nd: Devonshire House and *Mr.
Nightingale's Diary* on the 27th.   In the
London of that May-month, it was Dickens
and Thackeray, Thackeray and Dickens.
"Their names," wrote their young‧critic in
the *North British Review*, "almost necessarily
go together."

And here is Thackeray's letter to my
father, written eighty years ago:

KENSINGTON, *Tuesday, M.* 9.

"MY DEAR SIR,—I received the *N.B. Review* and am very glad to know the name of the critic who has spoken so kindly in my favor. Did I not once before see your handwriting in a note wh. pointed out to me a friendly notice of *Vanity Fair*—then not very well known or much cared for—and struggling to get a place in the world? If you were the author of the article to which I allude, let me thank you for that too; I remember it as gratefully as a boy remembers his 'tips' at school, when sovereigns were rare and precious to him. I don't know what to say respecting your present paper, comparisons being difficult, and no two minds in the least alike. I think Mr. Dickens has in many things quite a divine genius, so to speak, and certain notes in his song are so delighful and admirable that I should never think of trying to imitate him, only hold my tongue, and admire him. I quarrel with his Art in many respects, wh. I don't think represents Nature duly; for instance Micawber appears to me an exaggeration of a man, as his name is of a name. It is delightful and makes me laugh; but it is no more a real man than my friend Punch is; and in so far I protest against him—and against the doctrine quoted by my reviewer from Goethe too—holding that the Art of Novels is to represent Nature; to convey as strongly as possible the sentiment of reality—in a tragedy or a poem or a lofty drama you aim at producing different emotions; the figures moving, and their words sounding, heroically; but in a drawing-room drama a coat is a coat and a poker a poker, and must be nothing else according to my ethics, not an embroidered tunic, nor a great red-hot instrument like the Panto-mime weapon. But let what defects you (or rather I) will, be in Dickens's theory, there is no doubt according to my notion that his writing has one admirable quality—it is charming—that answers everything. Another may write the most perfect English, have the greatest fund of wit learning and so forth—but I doubt if any novel-writer has that quality, that wonderful sweetness and fresh-ness wh. belongs to Dickens. And now I have carried my note out of all bounds, and remain, dear sir, yours very faithfully,

"W. M. THACKERAY."

The years went by, and somehow, though my father knew Thackeray, he was never to know Dickens personally. Their only real meeting was on the famous evening at the Garrick Club—the old Garrick, in King Street, Covent Garden—when Dickens and Douglas Jerrold made up their quarrel. It had arisen out of some theatrical performance, in aid of a charity, and it had lasted for some time. On that evening, my father, with

Douglas Jerrold and some other friends—all fellow-members of "Our Club"—were dining at the Garrick with Humffreys Parry. Dickens and Albert Smith were dining at a small table quite near to them. Dickens and Douglas Jerrold, as it happened, were so seated as to be almost exactly back to back. All through dinner they had seemed oblivious of this fact; when suddenly Douglas Jerrold wheeled round in his chair and put his hand on Dickens's shoulder: "Charlie, my boy, how are you?" Dickens, wheeling round too, held out both his hands to Jerrold. Everybody was glad; and the two dinner-parties became one for the rest of the evening. I believe at the time it was thought by some people that the two dinners, and the back-to-back arrangement of Dickens and Douglas Jerrold, had been carefully planned and staged by their friends.

A year or two later my father was one of the mourners at Douglas Jerrold's grave in Norwood Cemetery; and he watched Dickens and Thackeray standing there together; Dickens with his hair blown back by the breeze, and Thackeray a little behind him, tall among the rest. That remained always my father's feeling about Thackeray—"A man apart—a head taller than any of his fellows." And he did come to know Thackeray fairly well. They were both members of "Our Club" in its most brilliant days, and often met there. *Macmillan's Magazine* and the *Cornhill* were for a year or two to run together, the two monthlies; my father editor of *Macmillan*, and the *Cornhill*— the younger magazine by two months—under the brilliant editorship of Thackeray. Then, on Christmas Eve 1863, came Thackeray's sudden death; and it fell to my father to write for the *Daily Telegraph*, all in a hurry, its leader on "The Present Condition of English Literature, *à propos* of the Death of Thackeray."

Dickens and Thackeray: the names of the two great Victorian novelists will always go together. Together, and yet always apart, they climbed, up and up, the hard rough climb to literary fame. Dickens, brave of heart, perhaps under a rather garish sun, reached his highest point, the watershed where, if a man be clear of vision, he may see the infinitesimal streamlets beginning to move downward the other way. To Thackeray it was given to climb, by as rough a track, "a man apart, a head taller than any of his fellows"; and, climbing still, still among the boulders, to be lost to us in the mists.

CHAPTER II

HOLMAN HUNT AND SIR ATALANTA

COVENTRY PATMORE, then one of the Librarians in the British Museum, took my father in the summer of 1847 to call on Mr. and Mrs. Charles Orme in Avenue Road, Regent's Park. My mother—their eldest daughter— was then a child; and the household consisted of the parents, their young family, and Mrs. Orme's two sisters. One of the sisters, Emily Andrews, had just become engaged to Coventry Patmore. She was the "Angel in the House" of his poem.

In this Avenue Road household my father found a little circle of literary friends. He always remembered meeting Emerson there one evening, when Emerson was on his second visit to England; and he remembered that, on this particular evening, Emerson's conversation turned to the subject of the *gender of Deity*, and that he told his audience how an American lady had been much troubled on this point, and how he had persuaded her to find spiritual satisfaction in the idea of an all-comprehensive It—"*It sees you.*"

My mother, the little eldest daughter, was in the room at the time; but she was too much of a child to remember any of Emerson's talk. She was, however, a little hero-worshipper; and very early next morning, before any of the household were astir, she stole downstairs and peeped into the deserted drawing-room, where the chairs were all standing as they had been left the night before, with the chair on which the American guest had been seated in the midst of the circle. It was the work of a moment for the child to turn this chair upside down, and with a big pin she scratched Emerson's name on the wooden bar underneath its damask seat; then she stole upstairs again. For a little while, childlike, she cherished her romantic secret; and then afterwards, childlike too, forgot all about it. Long years afterwards, when she was herself on a visit to her parents in the old home, and was sitting with a little circle about her in the old drawing-room, the talk happened to fall on the evening Emerson had spent there, and she suddenly remembered what she had done.

"I wonder," she said, looking about her at the chairs in the room, "which chair it was—I do believe you will find the name on one of them."

One by one the chairs were examined; and sure enough, on one of them was found the name, scratched in the childish writing—but the little hero-worshipper had spelt it **EMISON**. And Emison, in our family, the great American writer remains to this day.

Mr. and Mrs. Orme took a great and immediate liking to my father. His literary enthusiasms interested and stirred them. He told them about Aberdeen and Edinburgh; about Scott, and Burns, and the Disruption—all the things about which they knew so little, because they were things that had happened north of the Tweed. And to him, feeling rather solitary, living in rooms near the British Museum, and just beginning an uphill literary life in London, it was a rich new experience to be welcomed so warmly into this happy English home.

It was an early Victorian home. Every morning Mr. Orme, the soul of sunny punctuality, used to tap the weather-glass, and set off into town. There were no trains or tubes into the City in those days. The fact that he had returned home, in the late afternoon, was very often announced by the sound of the garden roller crunching the gravel paths in the square garden behind the house; a garden, and especially the gravel paths in it, of which he was extremely proud.

Mrs. Orme, who had married him when she was sixteen, was in 1847 not only the mother of young children, but the presiding genius of the home. Indeed, she seldom left it. When, as the years passed, those she loved "went wide in the world," she was content to follow them by writing to them, almost daily letters, at a little rosewood desk inlaid with mother-of-pearl, and plentifully stocked with pale pink "foreign" notepaper. Her interests were many. *The Times*, and the latest volume of Tennyson's Poems, lay always near to the little desk. The piano in the drawing-room was often open, but there was no music lying on it; for she had, in a wonderful degree, the gift of improvising her own and everybody else's accompaniments. Her music-master, for piano and organ, had been Charles Wesley; and among the songs of her girlhood had been Nathan's *Hebrew Melodies*, set to Byron's words. In the Avenue Road days, as her children were growing up, there never was such playing as hers—so delusive, so persuasive, so altogether dramatic—for their "drawing-room game" of Musical Chairs. There was never any

breakfast bell; but sometimes, when breakfast was more than ready and nobody had
come downstairs, she would open the piano
in the drawing-room and play, very softly
and tenderly, the first few bars of "Home,
Sweet Home!" She herself, if the morning
had been fine, would have been for quite a
long walk before breakfast, in the Hampstead
fields.

She was a wonderful hostess—really interested in hearing about other people's joys
and sorrows. The names of men and women
of her day — Victorians all — who gathered
round the hospitable dinner-table, or walked
on summer evenings in the Avenue Road
garden, are names still remembered in this
changed and changing world; or at any rate
can be looked up in the *Dictionary of
National Biography.*

It was a family habit, on summer evenings,
to walk in the garden in groups of twos and
threes, up and down the lawn, and round and
round the gravel paths under the pear trees.
William Michael Rossetti has described the
scene :

> " All calm, the dusk condenses round ;
>   The lawn is changing green to grey,
>   Our voices take a softer sound,
>   Light words are hushed we had to say,
>   And graver eyes peruse the ground."

In the early 'fifties the two young pre-Raphaelites, Holman Hunt and Thomas Woolner, were often of this little company. In the early 'fifties Rosaline Orme, who was a child when my father first came to the house, was seventeen. When she was eighteen, and he was a newly appointed professor at University College, they were married in the old Parish Church of Hampstead.

"Well I remember," wrote Holman Hunt to my mother not long before he died, "the days of Avenue Road. . . . I ever retain memory of the walk round the garden there, with Masson, when the fortunes of the P.R.B. looked most dismal (owing to the abuse of the Press) and the comfort his sympathy was to me. And, of course, I remember your happy wedding . . ."

In the summer before their marriage, the poor fortunes of the P.R.B. had sent Woolner to the Australian goldfields. Holman Hunt and his friend Edward Lear were living in a farmhouse near Hastings; Lear putting the limestone rocks into his " Quarries of Syracuse," and Holman Hunt painting his "Strayed Sheep " on the cliffs at Fairlight. Some brilliant butterflies had made their appearance in the Avenue Road garden—I think they must have been "Red Admirals," but there is no mention of the fact. The interest in them seems to have been purely æsthetic, and the butterfly hero of this story appears only as "Sir Atalanta."

"MY DEAR MISS ORME," Holman Hunt wrote from Clive Vale Farm. . . . "Your description of the lovely insects makes me wish greatly that you had been successful enough to catch one. I am intending to paint a butterfly in my picture, but have not yet caught any beautiful enough, and indeed have now, since the awful gales of the last week, given up the hope of seeing more.

"You speak of the delights of this blessed island with a warmth which, after six weeks' experience of rain, wind, dust, and bitter cold while painting on the top of Fairlight Cliff, I feel quite excused for not finding sufficient national pride left in me to feel. I used once to wonder whether England would ever be invaded; now I wonder that it was ever inhabited, and how much longer it will be before all the people leave for some reasonably temperate clime; before finishing this note I will endeavour to give you an idea of my position while painting, so that, if my want of patriotism appears shameful, you may judge me with proper consideration of the provocation received. I have made the sketch, and also another, a prophetic one, of painting in the East, as a set-off to yours. The lady in black is a daughter of a Greek merchant, lately dead, who has come with her cousin, the fair lady, to have her portrait painted with the gazelle, into which she believes her lover to have changed after his murder by her father. What do you think of the plot? You will allow that it has the merit of originality.

"With kind regards to Mr. and Mrs. Orme, Miss Andrews, and your brothers and sisters. —I remain, yours very sincerely,

W. HOLMAN HUNT."

With the letter came two pen-and-ink sketches, "Painting in England, Hastings 1852," and "Painting in the East, Grand Cairo 185–." "Painting in England" is a humorous sketch; the painter is huddled up on his cliff by the sea at Fairlight, trying to paint in the teeth of the wind. Pipe in mouth, he clutches his sketching-block with one hand, his pencil with the other. His coat-collar is turned up; his hat, blown off, is suspended in mid-air, attached by a cord to his coat-button. His umbrella, blown inside out, is poised vertically on the top of his head. One of the bathing-machine women of those days, an "ugly" tied over her bonnet, is leaning over him. "What a delightful h'art!" she is saying—the words are in a tag, out of her mouth. The cliffs are there, sloping to the water-edge; and behind them is the line of the sea.

The companion-sketch—the "prophetic one"—is not humorous. The scene is a courtyard in Cairo, a light arcading in the background, a fountain playing into a basin in the centre; and in this sketch the painter is at work at his easel, his palette on his thumb. The "fair lady" watches him at work, flirting her fan; and a black boy, kneeling, holds a big parasol over them both. On the marble steps at a little distance sits a beautiful and dejected figure—"the lady in black," oblivious of their presence. One or two gazelles have come about her, the head of the foremost gazelle is almost in her lap; his little tongue is licking her hand; her forehead is laid against his shoulder. The glamour of the East is in the picture—the East which the young painter was, even then, longing to see.

When the two sketches arrived in Avenue Road the summer was almost gone; but, by good luck, one butterfly remained—and was captured. Tenderly packed in a little box, punctured to let in the air, he went off by post to the farm at Fairlight.

"I do not know how to thank you enough," Holman Hunt wrote, "for your kindness in

sending the butterfly, which arrived quite
safely and in good health to-day. I will
take the very earliest opportunity of painting it, and, as I know your kind heart would
have, restoring it its liberty."

And another letter followed on October 1st.

". . . I was very pleased to find that my
lame note of the beginning of this week had
quieted your fears about poor butterfly, and
am very glad to be able to add more respecting the creature's further history of a satisfactory character.   Tuesday here gloried in a
most violent hurricane, therefore all I could
do was to increase its comfort while still a
prisoner.   So, with a clean box and fresh
flowers, this was done.   This morning being
finer, I put Sir Atalanta under a glass with a
flower, and commenced painting him, but
was soon compelled to stop in consequence
of the steam rendering his covering of too
opaque a nature to permit his beauty to be
seen: therefore I removed the tumbler, and
while he was venting his rage upon the pane
for being an invisible bar to his freedom, and
also while recovering from the exhaustion
resulting from each attack, I managed to
portray him in life-like, or rather Roberson's,
colours; being finished I took him on his
flower into the garden, and introducing his
attention to a large geranium, which he
examined with much more leisure than my
engagements and impatience would permit

me to consider, so I wafted him up into the air: there he jerked and tumbled about with the utmost vigour but seemed inclined to consider it all a joke, and so much the best way for his dignity to show that he was not to be deluded into an idea that he was free, until at last it entered into his shallow head that he might indeed be at liberty, and it might be worth while to fly away: so he flapped his wings for a forward flight, dodging all over the field and about the hedge and across the next field, amongst trees and weeds, in amongst ditches and stubble and haystacks, and lastly clean out of sight. So let us hope that he will have a long and happy life, and has escaped the horrors of this cold wretched night in some warm shelter known only to himself. I wonder whether he will go back to London to his friends, or be introduced into the select circles of butterflies of this district. Perhaps he can't talk Hastish, or Fairlish. Perhaps he's a Freemason, and can get on without talking. Who knows? . . ."

Holman Hunt painted the butterfly— poised on one of the little woolly heads in his picture "Strayed Sheep." I do not know on whose walls the butterfly's portrait hangs to-day. The two pen-and-ink sketches, each with the W.H.H. in the left-hand corner, hang in our house in Edinburgh; and on the same wall is some of Woolner's work—all done before he went to Australia. Madox Brown's "The Last of England" was inspired by Woolner's going; but it was not to be the last of England for the young sculptor, who came home and eventually found his place among the Victorian Royal Academicians.

CHAPTER III

A LONDON CHILDHOOD

STRANGE, the part that sound plays in the memories of one's childhood. There was the screech of a macaw, whose cage must have hung somewhere in the sunshine of one of the neighbouring gardens. More distant were the bugle-calls, mysterious and romantic, from the barracks in the Wellington Road; and more distant still—from far away it sounded, in the region of Portland Town— came, faintly pulsating on the hot summer air, the music of an old hand-organ that seemed to be always playing there, and always playing the same tune; infinitely sad and tender. Not till long afterwards did I know it to be the "*Ah, che la Morte*" of Verdi's *Trovatore*.

There was another, a quite different sound; but that came from the front of the house, and brought us children—the children of two nurseries under our grandfather's roof— round to the balconied windows, festooned with Virginian creeper, and the little sweep

of gravel, with the row of lime-trees between
the two gates that opened into the Avenue
Road.   It was a cry; a clear, ringing octave,
in a woman's voice:

"Any   new   milk   from   the   Countery
Coo—oo?"

A great brown cow came slowly and
heavily townwards along the middle of the
road, from the direction of the Swiss Cottage;
and walking by the cow was a milkmaid,
wearing a pink cotton sun-bonnet and carrying her milking-pail and stool.

We took a deep interest in the "countery
coo."   Once we saw a neat parlour-maid
come down the steps of a house nearly
opposite to ours, and present her jug to be
filled.   That was a thrilling moment when
the cow stopped, and the milking-stool and
pail were put in action, and then—the little
ceremony over — cow and milkmaid proceeded slowly on their way towards the
park gates and Baker Street; and again the
clear cry would sound—"Any new milk
from the Countery Coo—oo?"   A veritable
Kate Greenaway picture, before the days of
Kate Greenaway.

As far as I can remember, we never tasted,
nor wished to taste, that milk.   Ours was
a purely æsthetic interest.   The cows in St.

James's Park were quite another matter. They were historic—aristocratic cows. They were mixed up in our minds with a great deal about Oliver Cromwell, and a very little—but how delightful that little was!—about Charles II. It was of those cows, and the dusty crowd gathered about them in a space behind the Horse Guards, that we thought when we repeated, in all good faith, our nursery prayer:

> " Pity my Simple City,
> Suffer me to come to Thee ! "

It was a pleasant excitement to thread one's way, holding tightly to a grown-up person, through the crowd, on a hot summer day, when the patient beasts stood flicking their tails among the white stalls of gingerbread and carraway biscuits, and the bottled "pear-drops" melting in the sun. I do remember drinking a glass of milk in St. James's Park.

I sometimes wonder what the Faculty would say now to some of the happy-go-lucky methods that prevailed in our nursery days. Not that we were not well looked after; the Faculty, for us, was represented by the brisk and kindly doctor with grey side-whiskers, Mr. Musgrave, whose large family practice lay round about the Avenue Road. He

came, sometimes on foot, sometimes in his
one-horse brougham; and the grown-up
people knew and liked him so well that they
sometimes spoke of him as "Muzzy."

One of our periodical excursions "into
Town," two or three times a year, was to a
fine old eighteenth-century house in one of
the side streets off Regent Street. The
Parkinsons, father and son, had for genera-
tions been dental surgeons to the Royal
Georges; and in their consulting-room was
a glass case containing specimens of certain
Royal Georgian extractions, each with its
little biographical label attached. Our dread
of this consulting-room was mitigated by the
fascinations of the glass case, and by the
sponge-cakes at a confectioner's in Regent
Street before we were trundled home again.

Before the days of trains and tubes,
omnibuses were the method of conveyance;
and there were only two omnibuses running
—the light-green Atlas and the dark-green
City-Atlas. They were carpeted deep in
"fresh straw"; and, sitting in them, we
children used to amuse ourselves picking
out the long stems and examining the
threshed-out corn-ears, to see if by chance a
stray grain of corn might have been left by
"the Farmer" in one of the little pockets.

Very rarely, I believe, we did find one—and we ate it; solemnly dividing it, as far as possible equally, between us.

We had a speaking acquaintance with the "ripen'd ears" and the "happy Autumn-fields"; we had heard about William and Dora and the poppies. Tennyson's Poems were always being quoted in the house in Avenue Road; members of the Tennyson family were often there—their brilliant Tennysonian talk, unconventional and inspiring, has been handed down to us as a literary possession. But when, in our childhood days, we talked of "corn" we thought instinctively of the warm, deep straw inside a dark-green City-Atlas.

There was a fascination in those expeditions into Town; and yet I do not think we little Londoners saw any of the orthodox sights of London while we lived there. But we loved the Lowther Arcade; and in after-years Sir James Barrie's obituary notice of the dear place brought tears to the eyes, through which we beheld again our sawdust Paradise of wax-dolls and wooden-horses. We gazed reverently at Temple Bar, " Where the Heads used to stick on the Poles"—and privately we regretted they were not sticking there still. We knew the Diver and his great diving-bell at the Polytechnic; and we were deeply attached to a baby-mummy in the British Museum, the patient dignity of whose little face is graven on my heart to this day.

When we "went to the country"—to Hastings, or Tunbridge Wells—we drove in a four-wheeler to London Bridge. The cab, an odd-shaped wooden box on wheels, painted a loud red and green and lined with hot red velvet, was, like the omnibuses, carpeted thick with straw. It was driven by a typical London "Cabby" in shiny waterproof cape and hat, who came to fetch us, by special arrangement, all the way from Chalk Farm. Once packed into the cab we settled down resignedly for the long, jolting, uncomfortable drive; and we thoroughly disliked that part of it that took us through the City. There was no Victoria Embankment—the Thames, in the early 'sixties, was not by any means the salubrious river we know to-day. In the late 'fifties, during one particularly hot July, the state of the Thames was such that Parliamentary Committees could not sit in the rooms overlooking the river; and judges and juries were performing their duties "under a sense of danger," and hurrying away from the Courts as soon as possible.

It was even under consideration whether the House of Commons should not adjourn to some healthier part of London.

I can see my pretty young mother—she was born within the sound of Bow-Bells, and loved every inch of the City—looking out of the cab-window.

"Now, children," she would say, "Look; we are passing Bread Street, where Milton was born!"

But had we any intention of looking out of the cab-window, at Bread Street, where Milton was born? Not we; we were experienced travellers; we knew what was coming, and had laid our plans accordingly. We had our own theory about the peculiarly objectionable sweet odour that came up from the river-side at this particular part of the drive to London Bridge. We believed it to be caused by the baking of a very nasty kind of loaf which had given its name to Bread Street and was historically connected with Pudding Lane and Pie Corner—two other places, as we knew, in this unpleasant part of London. We were determined never to eat the loaf, the pudding, or the pie, and our mother's "Look, children, where Milton was born!" was quickly followed by her light laugh: "You little fastidious things!" For we had clapped our small pink-bordered cotton pocket-handkerchiefs over our noses; the pocket-handkerchiefs of those nursery days, bordered, for girls, with flower-baskets and garlands, and for boys, with wheelbarrows and jockeys on horseback.

After all, the long drives into the City happened only seldom. Our El Dorado lay in the opposite direction—"up the road," past the Swiss Cottage, and out towards Finchley, Hendon, Golders Green, and Hampstead Heath. The Swiss Cottage was then a dairy, with long, thatched roof and quaint little windows, in one of which was always a basket of eggs. And just beyond the Swiss Cottage the fields began, with the buttercups and the hawthorn hedges, and the ponds where we watched the tadpoles absorbing their tails for the purpose of turning into frogs. Aspens still trembled at the corner of Child's Hill Lane; Golders Green was still a Green, surrounded by white posts and swinging chains. Down Hendon way the old Cock and Hoop Inn was still in existence, with a stagnant pond in front of it, and a painted sign over its doorway—the Cock triumphant in a Golden Hoop.

Not long ago, finding myself in the Finchley Road, I made a little pilgrimage to look for the Cock and Hoop. I remembered the old days when we used to bowl our own hoops past its door, under its sign, looking up at the Cock and laughing, as we ran by. But I found myself in a new and strange world; a world of streets and shops. A young policeman was standing at a corner, and I appealed to him.

"Constable," I said, "can you direct me to an old inn called the Cock and Hoop?"

"*Cock and Hoop?*" He stared as if I had stepped out of another century—which indeed I had. And then a sudden look of kindliness came into the young man's face. "Ah!" he said; "that's like my grandfather! He belonged down hereabouts— never done talking about it! He thought the world of that old pub!"

A brick-red path slanted upwards across the Hampstead fields—a path with white stiles in it—towards the old town of Hampstead and the spire of its parish church.

In connection with white stiles, our grandmother taught us a very old song, handed down by her grandmother from a previous century:

" Ven Villiam at eve met me down by the stile
How sveet was the nightingale's song."

And she used to explain to us children that

the *V* for *W* was, at the time the song was fashionable at musical evenings in London, merely a little affectation in accordance with the pronunciation of a German-speaking Court.

CHAPTER IV

A PHILOSOPHER AT PLAY

OUR education was as desultory as it was delightful. Very early in my existence I was lifted on to a table to recite "Last May a braw wooer cam doon the lang glen" for the benefit of my father's colleague in University College, the dear old fellow-Scotsman, Dr Sharpey. And very soon after that I was standing at my father's knee, taking my first Latin lesson out of a small thin black volume called *Ruddiman's Rudiments*. I remember my father's gentle remonstrance at my manner of declining *Penna*, a pen, all in one breath:

"*Pnapnaepnaepnampnapna.*"

When first he presented me with *Ruddiman's Rudiments* he brought from his study one of his own quill-pens, to show me why the Latins used the same word for pen and feather. His students of later days may recall the advice he used to give them in his lectures on expository literature—"Exemplify: Exemplify."

37

We had a good many books: *The Fair-
child Family, Sandford and Merton,* Miss
Edgeworth's *Rosamond and the Purple Jar,
Robinson Crusoe,* Lamb's *Tales from Shakespeare,* and *The Arabian Nights*—this last in
a beautifully illustrated edition which we
were allowed to paint with an admixture of
honey with the water-colours—supposed to
give an Oriental effect. We read *Little
Arthur's History of England,* Jane Porter's
Scottish Chiefs, and *The Queens of England*
by Agnes Strickland and her sister. Our
mother read with us Ancient History and
Roman History, and took us to the British
Museum to see the mummies and the sculp-
ture. But the most precious of our nursery
literature emanated from the house of Macmillan. It was Alexander Macmillan who
brought me, one winter evening, in his coat-
pocket, a little dark-red leather Prayer-Book
with gilt clasp and corners; and it was he
who gave us the *Golden Treasury Fairy-book*
and the *Golden Treasury of Verse.*

Lying on the hearthrug we read, in their
beautiful English, the old fairy-tales in which
impossibilities are so close-knit with the
everlasting truths; and we soon knew by
heart many of the verses in Palgrave's
Golden Treasury edition. One of the young

writers who, back in the 'forties, had brought his poems to the house in Avenue Road was William Allingham. It was at the time when the Tennysons—Horatio and Matilda, the Rossettis—Christina and William Michael, and the two young pre-Raphaelites, Thomas Woolner and Holman Hunt, were also coming there, for sympathy in their work and in their young dreams. Some years later Allingham's *Fairies* had found their way into the *Golden Treasury of Verse*. They were the favourites of our nursery days. Playing on Hampstead Heath meant, for us, being Allingham's "Fairies"; and many a time did the solitary reaches of the Heath resound to shrill childish voices:

> " Wee folk, good folk,
>   Trooping all together,
> Green jacket, red-cap,
>   And grey cock's feather."

I do not suppose anybody to-day could imagine a picnic under the Pines at Hampstead; a real picnic, with white tablecloth and table-napkins, plates, and knives and forks, cold lamb and mint-sauce, chicken and salad, gooseberry puffs and cup-custard sprinkled with nutmeg. The very remembrance brings back with it the aromatic scent of those Giant Pines—not the Pines that are there to-day; and the scent of ripe strawberries in the hot sun, among the soft sand and the pine-needles. A girl used to stand there selling strawberries in long, pointed "pottles": a girl with a pottle slung over her arm, just like Sir Joshua Reynolds's "Strawberry Girl." And sometimes a gipsy-woman would appear on the scene; a woman with enigmatical, blazing dark eyes and a scarlet handkerchief tied over her dark head. Once our mother—in a straw bonnet and a fringed shawl with a "pine-apple border"—slipped off her wedding-ring, "crossed her palm" with silver, and listened, smiling, while the gipsy told her fortune. Afterwards our mother missed a pretty lace handkerchief, and was sorry because it was "one of a wedding set"; and we hunted long for it among the pine-roots. But it was never found again—and the gipsy-woman had dis-appeared too.

Always, before we left the Heath, we used to fill our own pocket-handkerchiefs with sand, from under the Pines, to carry home. It was a little ritual, and we never gave up hope; though always, before we reached home, the last grains of sand had run out, and the pocket-handkerchief was empty.

I remember one special picnic under the

Pines at Hampstead. We children must have come up in the usual happy cavalcade with the double perambulator; and our grandmother, with some of the grown-up people, drove, bringing the hampers—and Herbert Spencer. "Mr. Spencer the Philosopher," as we always called him, was often a guest at the house in Avenue Road; but only on this one occasion can I recall him in *al fresco* mood, sitting with a plate on his knees, among the sand and the pine-needles, eating cold lamb and salad, and arguing pleasantly all the time as to whether the æsthetic pleasures of a meal eaten out-of-doors in summer were of real assistance to the digestion. We children, listening—and eating gooseberry puffs—thought there was no doubt about it.

For a time the Coventry Patmores lived in a little cottage at North End, close to the Bull and Bush Tavern. It was, I think, one of the old wooden houses, and has long since been pulled down. Mrs. Patmore, the first wife, "the Angel in the House," who was my grandmother's younger sister, we knew as "Aunt Emily."

I remember spending an afternoon at Elm Cottage. Coventry Patmore—to our satis-

faction—was at the British Museum; and
Aunt Emily and her children came with us
a little way homewards across the Heath.
I can see her now, as she bade us good-bye in
the evening light, with the rough Heath
behind her, a Juno figure in her simple
brown dress. Her children had brought
with them a large red air-ball, a new possession; and the Angel in the House stooped to
whisper something to her little Emily, the
eldest girl, who, after her mother's death,
was re-baptised into the Church of Rome
and became a nun. Emily ran forward to
where I stood, put the string of the air-ball
into my hand, and then, with a sudden
gesture of happy renunciation, ran back
to her mother. As for us, we went home
with hearts as light as the air-ball.

The "Air-Ball Man" was quite an institu-
tion in those days. He used to come up
the Avenue Road calling "Air-Balls! Air-
Balls!" and our grandmother would lean
over the Virginian-creepered balcony and
buy a whole bunch of them—white, pink,
blue, and orange. "Mr. Spencer the Philosopher," if he found us playing (in the
drawing-room) with air-balls or with battle-
dores and shuttlecocks, would join quite
pleasantly in the game.

Our attitude to Herbert Spencer was one of friendly detachment. We knew—for we had been told—that he was a very clever man, who wrote books, especially one which was about the proper way to educate children. He certainly looked at us as if he thought we were worth noticing, and if he asked us a question he waited for the answer, as if he thought it might be worth hearing. He always had twinkling eyes and a whimsical smile, no matter to whom he was talking, so they did not mean that he was laughing at us. He was always talking—almost always arguing—and everybody in the room was interested in what he was saying, though they did not always agree with him. Sometimes we understood what it was all about. For instance, we understood about the importance of using the right words to express a meaning. Nobody in the Avenue Road household would ever have thought—in Herbert Spencer's presence—of asking for "half-a-cup more tea." If an unwary guest happened to do so, we were prepared for the brilliant Spencerian dissertation on accuracy of expression; on the folly of speaking of "half-a-cup," when in fact it was a whole cup half full. And in debate—even over a trifle—the Philosopher, with his twinkling eyes and his whimsical smile, was in earnest.

Quite seriously he practised trios at the piano: "Love in thine Eyes," and "The Minute-Gun at Sea." There is in this a very high-pitched "Hark! A Signal!" which so startled and distressed Herbert Spencer, that often, in order to soothe his ruffled susceptibilities, the trio would be abruptly ended, and the piano gently closed.

In earnest was he, too, when he played the game of croquet on the lawn behind the house. On hot days he would come provided with a large white umbrella, which he held over his head. When the moment came for him to play his stroke, he would hand the umbrella to the person who happened to be standing nearest to him. "Hold the umbrella! Hold the umbrella!" he would say; and after the stroke was made he would take back his umbrella—often from the hands of one of our very young and pretty aunts.

Only once can I recollect Herbert Spencer being attacked with his own weapons. It was, I think, on one of those Sunday evenings at home that for so many years attracted a brilliant little company of literary, artistic, and scientific friends to the house in Avenue Road. Herbert Spencer was sitting on a pale yellow damask sofa, against a wall-paper of grey-green, and he was surrounded by a half-circle of listeners. The talk had fallen on the pronunciation of the English language. Herbert Spencer was holding forth on a system of education which he had been trying on his landlady, a worthy but rather nervous person, with the result— a result he had been observing with some interest—that she seemed to be losing the power of accentuation; she had begun, out of sheer nervousness, to lay the accent on the wrong words and syllables of words. I cannot remember the exact examples he gave, but they were something of this kind. The simple question "Are you dining at home to-night, Mr. Spencer?" would be rendered, "Are *you* dining *at* home to-night, Mr. Spen*cer*?"

The group of listeners was suddenly startled by the voice of one of the very young and pretty aunts. She, who had so often held the umbrella dutifully over the Philosopher's head, was speaking, quietly but distinctly, looking at him with wide-open grey eyes. "Mr. Spencer, you are an inhuman monster!"

There was a moment's hush, and then

a ripple of appreciative laughter, in which Herbert Spencer himself very heartily joined. He seemed really pleased.

In after years, Herbert Spencer visited us in Edinburgh and in the Vale of Yarrow, where we spent an autumn holiday, and where he brought not only his umbrella, but his fishing-rod.

For a time Herbert Spencer lived in a house of his own in Avenue Road, and on one of our visits to London we lunched with him there. With his old-world courtesy and hospitality he talked quite tenderly of the old days, and he insisted, I remember, on producing at lunch some rather precious "gaudy ale." And once again, when I was in London, he took me—with a fine disregard of all club rules—into the billiard-room of the Athenæum. It was his El Dorado; and I keep this, my last memory of our "Mr. Spencer the Philosopher," as a very happy one.

CHAPTER V

EVENINGS AT AVENUE ROAD

AMONG the friends who, in our childhood days, were most often present on those Sunday evenings were the Forbes-Robertsons, the Garnetts, the Hemmings, and the Lockyers; all of them young then, and with young children of their own.

Mr. and Mrs. Forbes-Robertson—father and mother of Sir Johnston—were exceptionally beautiful to look at, very artistic and literary, altogether wide and human in their sympathies, and dear friends of our family. Dr. Garnett of the British Museum was a veritable treasure-house of literary information, which he was always ready to impart with a rapid lucidity peculiarly his own; and with all his knowledge he was a most self-deprecatory *savant*. He and Mrs. Garnett used to walk over on Sunday evenings from their house on Primrose Hill. He was a faithful friend of my father's; but I did not know until the other day, when I was reading one of his son's delightful reminiscent papers in *Maga*, that the three portraits that always hung on the walls of Dr. Garnett's study were those of Shelley, de Quincey, and David Masson. When, in the 'eighties, Dr. Garnett received the LL.D. of Edinburgh University, he and Mrs. Garnett stayed with us. Mrs. Garnett, in her pretty intimate manner, told us she had felt it an occasion when she ought to wear her wedding-dress; and this she did —and very charming she looked in it, re-adapted to the fashion of the moment—at a little dinner-party my parents gave in their honour.

The Hemmings lived beyond the Swiss Cottage. I have a childish memory of their house in Fairfax Road; of Mrs. Hemming's unruffled sovereignty, her exquisite neatness and repose; and the orange-coloured bear-skin rug, which seemed deep to our small feet, in front of the drawing-room fireplace. Mr. Hemming, the very eminent barrister of Lincoln's Inn, who in those days had been Senior Wrangler and was going to be Q.C., was regarded by us children with a mixture of awe and pity; for we had been told that he was such a "tremendously hard worker" that, after being busy all day at the Courts, he "had to sit up writing all night." Our own father sometimes did this; but only, I think, when the monthly number of *Macmillan's Magazine* was coming out.

The Lockyers were also near neighbours. Mrs. Lockyer, Sir Norman's first wife, was very musical; her grand piano was the chief piece of furniture in their little drawing-room; and even in those old-young days there was a telescope on the roof of Norman Lockyer's house.

But I must not forget Professor and Mrs. Bain of Aberdeen. Alexander Bain and my father were old friends; they had been boys together in Aberdeen; and when Bain was living in London in the early 'fifties, working with John Stuart Mill and lecturing at the new Bedford College for Women, he came often to the house in Avenue Road. He married the Lady Principal of Bedford College; and after that both of them, through all the years, whenever they visited London, used regularly to make their appearance at my grandparents' house. The family annals include one or two stories of Alexander Bain in his younger days.

Our mother, one of the first pupils of Bedford College, attended his lectures on geography; and very splendid lectures, she used to say, they were. They were given at an early hour in the morning; and sometimes she would meet the lecturer hurrying through the park gates; and he always greeted her in exactly the same words:

"It's the earrly birrd that gets the worrm, Miss Orrme!"

He was a great and discursive talker at the Avenue Road dinner-table, and he would sometimes forget, in the interest of the talk, to go on eating.   My grandmother, by way of gentle reminder, would ask:

"Won't you—have a little—more?"

"Later, Mrs Orme—later!" he would say, without even looking at the plate before him. It is recorded that once he was heard to reply, "Later, Mrs Orme—considerably later!"

Perhaps I ought to explain the mention of the yellow damask sofa and grey-green wall-paper in the drawing-room of my grand-parents' house.   The room had originally been furnished according to the taste of the young pre-Raphaelite, Thomas Woolner. When somebody spoke rather scornfully of the damask sofas and window curtains as "mustard colour," Woolner had flashed out, "But mustard is a very beautiful colour!" So mustard it remained.   The same shade was afterwards called "Old gold"; and there was a certain charm in the pre-Raphaelite blend of mustard and grey-green.   Woolner's statuette of "Love" stood (I am afraid it was under a glass shade) on the white marble mantelpiece; and the light of many candles shone down on it, their beams refracted by the crystal pendants of a "chandelier." To us, children of the early 'sixties, the chandelier hanging from the ceiling of that drawing-room was the last word in light.

I wish I could remember, accurately enough to write down, any fragment of the brilliant talk to which we children were so generously allowed to listen. I remember only enough of it—rapid thrusts of wit and argument, sudden flashes of real feeling—to make me somehow mistrust the modern word "conversationalist," so unwieldy and indefinite, which yet is so often on the lips of to-day.

One other memory I must record of those Sunday evenings at home. Sometimes, late in the evening, the piano would be opened for our mother to sing;—songs not often heard to-day. Perhaps one or two of the men would already have gone into the smoking-room for a cigar, before everybody said good-night and went away. But at the first sound of my mother's voice the smoking-room door would softly open, the fragrance of my grandfather's cigars would

steal out into the hall; the men had come
back, to stand listening in the darkness
outside the drawing-room.

Fellow-conspirators, we children felt them;
for we, too, late as it might be, sometimes
had crept from our nursery cots upstairs,
and were sitting on the lowest step of the
dark staircase listening to "*Lascia ch'io
Pianga*"; "Softly sighs the voice of evening"; "Tears, idle tears"; "O rest in the
Lord."

CHAPTER VI

MAINLY ABOUT THE CARLYLES AND MAZZINI

IT was for us a great event when we moved into a house in the Finchley Road; one of a row of villas looking straight on to the hayfields, with a strip of half-reclaimed land by way of garden behind it, where we found one or two white raspberries and plenty of frogs. I do not think there were any houses beyond that little row of villas, which has long since been demolished to make room for one of the Metropolitan railway stations.

Some memories belong to the two years we spent in this house, before we migrated to Edinburgh. In the spring of 1863 there had been the marriage of the Prince and Princess of Wales, and London's illuminations had been followed by various public appearances and occasions. But only one of these came our way. Earl Granville's farm lay somewhere up towards Finchley, and one summer day the young Prince and his beautiful bride were the guests at a garden-party there.   Market-garden carts, open carriages and perambulators were drawn up along the hedges of the Finchley Road, and children with their nursemaids—we among them—peeped curiously through gaps in the hedges at the gaily coloured, moving parasols, as the little groups of polite Victorian "ladies and gentlemen" walked about the rose-garden of Earl Granville's farm.

Thackeray died on Christmas Eve 1863, and sometime on Christmas Day my father received a hurried note—sent by hand—from Mr. Edward Levy (afterwards Mr. Levy Lawson, and later Lord Burnham), the proprietor of the *Daily Telegraph*.   The note was found, long afterwards, among my father's papers.   It asked him to "do for us to-day a leader on the present condition of English Literature, *à propos* of the Death of Thackeray."   And there was a postscript:

"The bearer will walk about the country till you tell him to return for copy."

Our family annals have handed down the story of that little Printer's Devil, and how he spent his Christmas evening in our house in Finchley Road.   He may, in obedience to his employer, have taken a walk about the wintry Hampstead or Kilburn fields, but he most certainly came back long before my father had finished his leader on the condition of English literature. It was quite late at night; my father was still writing; my mother sitting with him, listening to the familiar quill on his paper, when the parlour-maid looked into the study. "Please, ma'am," she said, "the Devil has been sitting by the kitchen fire all the evening, and cook says, hadn't she better give him some hot supper now?"

One evening Mr. Lockyer invited us to look at the moon through the telescope on the roof of his house. His explanation of what we were looking at contained the word "extinct," a word heard by us for the first time. After each of us in turn had looked through the telescope for the allotted number of minutes we compared notes and found we were all secretly agreed that it was just possible Mr. Lockyer might be mistaken; that it was just possible there might be people in the moon; in fact, even in the limited time allowed us for observation, we thought we had made out some weird, shadowy forms, slinking about the dark mysterious edges of those things he called "extinct," but which looked to us uncommonly like the margin of our willow-shaded, tadpole-populated pond in the Hampstead fields.

On another evening our parents were invited to look at the moon, and on that occasion Tennyson was there too. My father used to describe how everybody stood back in silence, waiting to hear the first words that should fall from the Poet Laureate's lips after he had finished looking at the moon. He looked at it for a long time, with Norman Lockyer at his side, explaining, in his quick, brilliant way, what he ought to look for and what he might expect to see. At last— "Ha!" he ejaculated with a deep Tennysonian laugh—"What becomes of the County Families now!"

We spent a memorable day on Wimbledon Common when the London Scottish—Lord Elcho the Colonel—was in camp there. We, and our very animated French *bonne*, were handed over into the charge of an orderly sergeant, who took us on a tour of inspection, not only of our father's tent, but of all the other little white tents, each set in its miniature garden plot of yellow gravel, scarlet geraniums, and blue lobelia. We walked about among the shooting-ranges and the targets; were taught the meaning of a "bull's-eye"; sniffed the hot air, laden with

the smell of gunpowder; and were allowed
to pick up one or two spent bullets to carry
home in our pockets. The sergeant probably enjoyed the occasion as much as we did;
and he ended by taking Henriette and her
charges into a big tea-tent. The climax
was reached when the sugar was stirred into
the tea-urn with a real dirk.

The shades of evening were falling on the
sun-baked Common when we were taken back
to our mother. The pipes were playing:
a huge ring of spectators was forming. One
of the London Scottish, who was a famous
dancer, was going to dance the sword-
dance.

"Run and say thank you, dear," my
mother whispered to me when it was ended.
An awful moment! I ran across the grass to
where he was standing by his crossed swords
—the spectators cheering him wildly. My
breathless "Thank you very much!" had an
unexpected result; for I was suddenly lifted
high on to a shoulder, carried—amid increased
applause—round the entire ring, and then set
gently down again at my mother's side.

It must have been soon after we went to
live in the Finchley Road that Mazzini and
Mr. Stansfeld (afterwards Sir James Stansfeld) came to call on my father and mother.

Both were old friends. My father's friendship with Mazzini dated from the days before Mazzini was one of the Triumvirs of Rome. My father had been for a year or two the first secretary of the Society of the Friends of Italy; Mazzini had been present at the marriage of my parents in the old Parish Church of Hampstead; had signed his name in the vestry afterwards, and then slipped away from the church door. Ten years later, much that the real "Friends of Italy" had worked so hard for was—or was being—accomplished. In April 1864 General Garibaldi's entry into London assumed "the character of a royal progress"; but at that time Mazzini, still refugee and propagandist, was again in trouble. For there had been discovered a conspiracy to assassinate Napoleon III.; and Greco, one of the Italians arrested, had stated that it was Mazzini who had suggested the assassination and supplied the money, bombs, and weapons. Mazzini's friend, James Stansfeld—Member for Halifax and Junior Lord of the Admiralty—was also implicated, because a paper had been found in the possession of another of the arrested conspirators, directing him to write to a certain "Mr. Flowers" at Stansfeld's own private address in London. There was dis-

cussion in the House of Commons. Stansfeld indignantly repudiated the charges
against himself, and maintained that Mazzini
had been cruelly and wrongfully accused;
but, though Lord Palmerston accepted the
explanation as "perfectly satisfactory," the
Member for Halifax, in March 1864, resigned
his office as Junior Lord of the Admiralty.

I wish I could date this visit of Mazzini
and Mr. Stansfeld to our father and mother.
Looking back, I think 'it must have been
either just before or just after Stansfeld's
resignation. I was in the room, and can
remember Mazzini talking vehemently, walking up and down as he talked, while Mr.
Stansfeld sat leaning back in his chair,
listening with a smile on his face to what
Mazzini was saying—perhaps he had heard it
all before. My parents were listening too;
and I—rather scared—had taken refuge under
the drawing-room table, an oval table with
a pedestal leg. Every now and then, Mazzini, walking round about the table, saw me,
and clapped his hands at me, with an "I
got you!" till someone—Stansfeld, I think—
said something to him in an undertone,
which I only half-heard, about its being "a
clear case of imprisonment." Mazzini, with
a laugh, desisted—and I, seeing my oppor-

tunity, escaped from under the table, and ran out of the room.

It is my only memory—faint but indelible —of the Italian patriot, of whose friendship my father has written, and of which he always spoke, as "one of the friendships of my life, for which I thank Fate, and which I shall ponder till I die."

One day when my father had gone into Town a carriage drove up to our gate. There was a little delay as the visitors got out and came slowly up the little path to our front door. My mother ran out to meet them; for it was Carlyle and Mrs. Carlyle—very frail she was then—who had driven over from Chelsea to call, quite unexpectedly. My mother took them into the dining-room, and put Mrs. Carlyle into one of the arm-chairs by the fire, in which she sat back in a kind of dreamy somnolence, while Carlyle, in the arm-chair opposite, did all the talking. He always liked talking to my mother; and on this occasion he was speaking, with all his accustomed fervour, of some heroic feat —I think it must have been something that was being reported in the newspapers of the day,—and my mother called it "an example of British pluck."

The word brought down a torrent of wrath

upon her head. *"Pluck!"* Carlyle ex-
claimed. Did Mrs. Masson know the meaning
of that word? *Pluck*—had she seen it, the
real thing, hanging outside of a butcher's
shop, gory and dripping. . . .

Mrs. Carlyle roused herself from her
lethargy. "Carlyle! Carlyle!" she said, in
a tone of weary remonstrance, "No doubt
Mistress Masson well knows the *abhorrent
mass!"*

Carlyle gave one of his laughs, and changed
the subject. Mrs. Carlyle had leant back
again in her chair, and spoke no more.

This was the only time I ever saw Mrs.
Carlyle. Carlyle himself we were often to
see again after our migration to Edinburgh.

One of the first letters that followed us to
Edinburgh was a sad little letter of good-bye
from him. He had called at the house in
Finchley Road; but, mistaking the day of
our departure, had gone a day too late, only
to find the house shut up and desolate; a few
straws or wood-shavings from the packing-
cases blowing about the house door in the
November wind.

When the letter came we were already in
the Royal Hotel in Princes Street, and our
father was making acquaintance with his
colleagues of the Edinburgh University of

1865. Campbell Fraser was an old friend;
Sellar, Blackie, and Tait also were to be
fellow-professors in the Faculty of Arts.   Sir
David Brewster, the Principal, was an old
man then, and I think at that time invalided
and abroad;   but I remember our father
telling us it was the Principal of the University who had invented our favourite toy—
the Kaleidoscope.   This seemed to give us a
proprietary interest in Sir David Brewster—
whom, as it happened, we children never saw.
We did not then dream of the years in front
of us, and the friendship to be given to us by
other, succeeding Principals of the University,
and their wives and families.   I remember
Sir   Alexander   and   Lady   Grant's   first
coming;   and Lady Grant—a grand-daughter
of "Christopher North"—proclaiming, with
a charming laugh, how glad she was, after
the luscious fruits of India, to taste "a real
Scotch ripe gooseberry again."   And with
them came the Dowager Lady Grant, a
stately figure, one hand on her son's arm, the
other holding her ebony stick.

When Sir William and Lady Muir arrived
among us—also from India—they caused
something of a sensation by sending a man-
servant on horseback to shower their cards
of invitation.   The little horse clattered

lightly up our front-door steps, to allow its rider to drop the big envelope into the letter-box.

My father had resigned his chair before Sir William Turner became Principal. In this case there was no arrival, for Sir William and Lady Turner and their family had long been in, and of, the University of Edinburgh. And then—it seems only yesterday—we were living through the anxious days of the Great War—when Sir Alfred and Lady Ewing arrived in Edinburgh. Some of us remembered Sir Alfred in the late 'seventies, when he was working with Professor Jenkin in our University. When he returned as its Principal, Edinburgh scarcely realised—I think Sir Alfred did not allow us to realise—the momentous things that had been, and were still, occupying him at the Admiralty, in that mysterious, now historic, "Room No. 40." Perhaps we should never have been allowed to realise them, if Lord Balfour himself had not divulged the secret.

CHAPTER VII

EDINBURGH AND THE HIGHLANDS

WE learnt a new word when we came
to Edinburgh—the word "acclimatised."
People, in the University and out of it, were
immensely kind; and almost everybody who
called on my mother asked her the same
question—looking rather anxiously for the
answer:

"And are you feeling acclimatised yet,
Mrs. Masson?"

My recollection is vague as to the severity
of that first winter. We began it in the
Royal Hotel in Princes Street, where Mr.
MacGregor, the proprietor, did everything
possible to make each one of us feel at home.
He was very pleased that my father had
chosen his hotel as our first "roof" in Edinburgh; and some time afterwards he sent
my mother, in recognition of this, a large
and beautiful MacGregor clan brooch, specially made for her acceptance. Then, for a
little while, till my parents could move into
their own house in Rosebery Crescent, we

were in rooms in Castle Street; and very strange we little Sassenachs felt there, in the charge of an elderly Highland nurse who had been recommended by Edinburgh friends: a very different type of nurse from the soft-hearted Lydia we had left on the platform at King's Cross, weeping, but afraid to venture, even with us, into a "foreign country."

The Highland nurse did not altogether approve of us; and indeed I think we must have bewildered her. For the first time in our lives, we found ourselves severely repri-manded. It was on a Sunday afternoon. Our parents were out, and we had been left sufficiently happy. It was tea-time, and my small brother was indulging in some very innocent antics round about the tea-table, when he was abruptly pulled up by a High-land voice in remonstrance:

"What! would you use your legs upon the Lord's Day?"

To both of us this was a question for debate; but I think from that day forward we neither of us fleeted the time quite so carelessly as we had done in the golden age.

And there were other lessons. Our first walks, as winter melted into spring, were out west towards Corstorphine and into the fields. Once, on the edge of a fascinating potato crop, we dug up a few little "new potatoes," tied them into our pocket-handkerchiefs, and proudly carried them home. This time it was our mother who expostulated. Gently but firmly she explained to us the meaning of "ownership of land"; incidentally, I think, she mentioned the words "stolen property." Anyhow, she said we were to go back next day and put the potatoes "exactly where we had found them." And we did.

I do not recollect what views our Highland nurse took of this incident—after all, she may have felt it to be a poor little raid, as raids go; but I have a vivid recollection of another excursion with her, in the spring or summer of that year. We were to be taken "a nice country walk," and had been provided with little packets of sandwiches for lunch. We set out in the direction of Gorgie, then less built over than it is to-day; but we did not get very far, for we were taken into a cemetery, and there enjoined to read, one after another, the deep-cut inscriptions on the stones. This we did obediently enough; but when it came to sitting down and untying our little packets of sandwiches among the flat tops of the tombstones, we rebelled. Such a picnic, to our minds, was neither reverential nor salubrious; and we turned resolutely homewards. I do not remember what we said when we reached home, but we made it clear that we were never to be asked to go for "that kind of picnic" again. And we never were.

At the beginning of April Carlyle came to Edinburgh to be installed Lord Rector of Edinburgh University. The Rectorial election, which had given Carlyle 657 votes to Disraeli's 310, must have happened just before we left London in November; but Carlyle's sad little note of good-bye that had followed my father, and had reached him at the Royal Hotel, did not, I think, mention the election. His installation as Lord Rector, with the extraordinary enthusiasm of his reception, his extemporaneous address, "full of his old fire and originality," was the great event in my father's first year in Edinburgh University.

While Carlyle was in Edinburgh he stayed with Erskine of Linlathen; but he and his brother John spent the evening before his Rectorial Address with my father and mother, "that he might have a quiet smoke" and talk over what he was expected to do and say next day. He was a little dubious as to how he might get through his ordeal. And

after the ordeal was over, one of the dinners
in his honour was at our house—followed by
a larger evening gathering. At the dinner-
table Lord Neaves sang his "Stuart Mill on
Mind and Matter " to the tune of "Roy's
Wife of Aldivalloch"; and Carlyle actually
joined, with his own voice, in the chorus.
There was a dinner given to him by the
Senatus Academicus in the Douglas Hotel,
at which the Principal, Sir David Brewster
—an old friend of Carlyle's—presided; and
Douglas Maclagan, the "academic laureate,"
sang his matchless songs.

It seemed but a few days afterwards, when
Carlyle was no longer in Edinburgh, but
people were still talking of the Rectorial
Address, that the news came of Mrs. Carlyle's
tragically sudden death in London—while
Carlyle was still away from home.

Autumn came—for us the first of many
glorious Highland autumns. Professor and
Mrs. Campbell Fraser and my father and
mother joined forces, and together took
Airdsbay House, on Loch Etive, for August
and September. It was a great exodus,
with the luggage and the domestic staffs of
both families; and the journey was not so
easy then as it is now. Mrs. Fraser's Highland cook was left at the ferry—almost in the

ferry—far into the night, negotiating, in
Gaelic, the transit of all our worldly goods.
Our own Highland nurse, once there, revealed
a character and an eloquence hitherto un-
suspected by us. In a very few days we
little Londoners had become passionately
Celtic and permanently barefooted. That
wonderful August and September! Ben
Cruachan's great head, albeit wrapped in
mists, dominated us day and night. Loch
Etive, in sunshine or gloom, will always be
to me, in memory, the most lonely and
beautiful of lochs. The big four-oared boat
and the little two-oared boat were always
waiting, ready—the sound of the lap-lap of
the salt water against their sides; and on the
sea-weedy shores the seals slept on the rocks.
How often we children used to steal barefoot
across the sea-weed and watch and listen for
the soft plash of a seal, slipping off a rock into
the clear brown waters of Loch Etive!

For the first time in our lives we saw
cream—thick, rich cream—in quart bottles,
and oat-cakes, warm from the girdle, spread
with fresh butter and home-made strawberry jam. And the apples! Not very far
away, reachable by boat, there was a Manse
orchard, where apples of all colours and
flavours literally fell into a child's lap.

So it was we came to understand the other facet of the word "acclimatised."

There was, of course, a rougher side to the Highland life of these beautiful glens. It was strange to see the older women, with their grey heads and weather-burnt faces, sitting over their fires smoking their black "cutty-pipes." Catering for a family on the shores of Loch Etive was, in those days, no easy matter, especially for a Londoner. My mother always remembered a day when she had ordered ducks for dinner; they arrived, certainly, in time to be roasted; but they came alive, and she was called to see—and hear—them waddling about the kitchen.

And in those beautiful surroundings there were signs—visible even to us children—of poverty and drink.

One day—a stormy day of sweeping wind and rain—there came in at the open door a woman, ragged and dishevelled, her black hair blown over her face and shoulders, her voice something between a skirl and a whine. My mother held out to her a shilling; and the woman, taking it, flung it with indescribable violence on to the stone floor. Lifting her hand high over her head she cursed everybody under the roof of Airdsbay House, and then suddenly turned and fled out into the wind and rain again.   Our Highland servants explained that she was angry because, of course, money was of no use to her: what she wanted was—tea, perhaps, and whisky, certainly.   The shilling was cruelty.

I believe it was not very long after our first autumn holiday that our mother invested in a copy of Adam Smith's *Wealth of Nations*, and imparted some of its wisdom to us children.

A friend of my father's—"Clark of Cambridge," as we had always heard him called —stayed with us at Airdsbay House.   He was then Public Orator, was editing the Cambridge edition of Shakespeare, and he was a contributor to *Macmillan's Magazine*; so he and my father had plenty to talk about. I don't recall that he had anything to say to us children; but he was still with us, I think, when there arrived another—to us more interesting—celebrity, who was as it happened also a Trinity College Cambridge man.   He arrived quite unintentionally, and was warmly welcomed at Airdsbay House.

It was one evening when we were all at the front of the house—a lovely evening, the loch was just beginning to take on its softer shades.   Somebody called attention to a tiny speck far out on the waters of the loch, where certainly no speck had been visible before. And as we watched, it grew bigger; it seemed to be coming nearer; surely it was not a boat? And yet, a boat it must be; a boat—of sorts; almost, it seemed, a live thing. . . . And then, suddenly, it shot into view. A canoe. A canoe on Loch Etive! A fling of a paddle, a glitter of water drops, and my father cried out, "I believe it's Macgregor—Rob Roy Macgregor—in his canoe!" A moment or two later he was standing among us, laughing, and everybody was shaking hands with him. Then he took up the little canoe, balanced it lightly on his shoulder, and walked with us up to the house.

We were all sorry when Rob Roy Macgregor said good-bye next morning; and we all turned out to see him depart. He asked —rather mischievously—if anybody would like to "try the canoe." My father shook his head; but Professor Campbell Fraser, long-limbed and long-bearded, volunteered. He managed, with some difficulty, to fit himself in. I think somebody handed him the paddle; but in another moment he and the canoe had turned turtle, and the Philosopher was in the water.

CHAPTER VIII

GIANTS OF THOSE DAYS

I HAVE one or two memories of our second Edinburgh winter. Sir George Grove (not then Sir George) came to see my father. The visit may have been in connection with my father's giving up the editorship of *Macmillan's Magazine*. One or two guests had been asked to dinner, and after dinner I was in the drawing-room, sitting on an inconveniently low chair with a very tall back to it,—a chair which was always kept well out of the way, in case an unwary guest might select it. I was listening to the conversation, and thinking that our visitor was much more like the friends we had left in London than the new friends around us in Edinburgh; much more like, for instance, Sir Norman Lockyer (not then Sir Norman), who had walked up and down the platform of King's Cross Station, holding us children by the hand till the very last moment before our train started.

And while these thoughts were occupying

me, Sir George Grove came across the room
and began to talk to me. I stood up—
Victorian children did that sort of thing.
But he said kindly, "No, no! You mustn't
do that; *you* must be sitting down, and *I*
must be standing by you, talking to you—
so!"

He laid an arm on the tall back of the
chair, on which he had re-seated me, and
himself stood, in an attitude of polite attention. I was too shy to do anything but
obey. We must have looked as if we were
posed for an early Victorian photograph;—
I can almost hear the photographer, "Now;
I am going to count three,—and pray do not
laugh!" But I have never forgotten our
little talk—or rather Sir George Grove's, for
he did all the talking.

"So!" he said, when we were both arranged
to his satisfaction. "What shall we talk
about?—Let's talk of something we both
know about. Let's talk about—London."

And then, at once, he saw that he was
talking to a child homesick for London; and
he went on rapidly:

"At least, let's talk about the railway
journey between London and Edinburgh. I
always enjoy a railway journey, don't you?
Especially stopping at York; the Refresh-

ment Room, you know; the tea and buns there are so good. I always enjoy the tea and buns at York, don't you?"

My memory carries me no farther; but, in a long life, I have never forgotten Sir George Grove's cheerful kindliness, and his "Let's talk of something we both know about."

My next memory is of an incident that might have had a serious ending.

A younger sister of my mother's was staying with us, and my mother had given a little dance—a very pleasant, quite informal dance. The guests were only just gone, at a very early hour in the morning, when my mother was called downstairs to see one of the maids who had been taken ill. So seriously ill did she seem, that my mother sent at once for the very nearest doctor; and when he came—it was still quite early in the morning—he thought, from the symptoms, and from their sudden onset, that it might be typhus fever. Of course it mightn't be, but he advised the immediate removal of the maid; and he himself sent word to the Infirmary—the old Infirmary with its wards of countless memories, which include the memory of Henley and Louis Stevenson. There was no great Royal In-

firmary in the Meadows then, and no great
City Hospital for Infectious Diseases out
beyond Morningside.

We were gathered for a late breakfast in
the dining-room, when from the bow-window
we saw a strange cavalcade draw up outside
our door. Two strong hospital porters,
heavily leathered-braced, were standing beside a most extraordinary object—something
between an eighteenth-century sedan-chair
and a Punch and Judy Show. It stood on
four legs. It had two poles sticking out,
back and front; and it was draped with
curtains of a faded blue and white cotton
that flapped uneasily in the wind.

A "Fever-Chair" had arrived, to carry our
poor maid away. It was an awful sight.

But almost simultaneously with the Fever-
Chair, there came up to the door two young
men, smiling and alert. They were two of
the guests who had been at the dance; who
had called out a light-hearted "Good night!"
on our doorsteps only an hour or two before.
They had heard at the hospital of our sorry
plight, and they had come themselves.
Briskly they superintended the removal.
The porters took up their burden. The
blue and white curtains were drawn. The
cavalcade moved off. Mrs. Masson need not

be in the least alarmed; everything would be done; very likely it would turn out not to be typhus; and in any case——

It did turn out not to be typhus; and in any case the patient — who made a good recovery — was in the very best possible hands that morning; for the two young men who had danced, and said good night, and come again so quickly, were to be very eminent physicians indeed, in after years. One was Sir Thomas Lauder Brunton who, in that winter, was Resident Physician at the Infirmary, and a student in my father's class in the University; and the other, I have always been told, was Sir David Ferrier.

Yet one more memory of those winter months. The Italian Opera was in Edinburgh, and my mother took me to hear the *Huguenots*. She had heard in London most of the operas in which Grisi and Mario sang together; and there was in Avenue Road a house with tall poplars about it, where, for a season or two, brilliant musical parties were given, when Grisi and Mario sang duets together. On those evenings the inhabitants of Avenue Road, if they chanced to be walking past the open lamp-lit windows of the house among the poplar trees, might listen to the most beautiful operatic singing in the world.

When the Italian Opera came that winter to Edinburgh, Mario's "velvet tenor" was past its prime, and Grisi was no longer singing in opera: Tietjens was the *prima-donna*, in her parts. But that evening Grisi was in one of the boxes. My mother whispered to me that I might look up and see her, sitting there alone. And after Mario's singing of "*Tu m'ami*," when the whole house was applauding enthusiastically, Mario looked up at the box, too, with an indescribable little gesture, as if he were going to kiss his hand. But Grisi shook her head, in smiling disapproval, and he desisted. It was an interesting little *entr'acte*, probably unnoticed by an enthusiastic audience.

The Edinburgh University coterie of that time was much smaller—perhaps for that very reason not less brilliant—than it is to-day. My father found himself one of the fine old, all-sufficient Seven of the Arts Faculty; and there were giants in all the Faculties. But I think everybody was—I know my father was, for one,—proud of our great Medical School; and I am glad that my picture gallery of childhood memories includes some of its great men.

There is in that picture gallery the severe old face and towering figure of Sir Robert Christison; there is the lion-headed Sir James Y. Simpson, an old man too, sitting in his arm-chair by the fireside in his house in Queen Street. I can hear his words to me: "Ye'll always remember, my dear, that ye've sat on the knee of the inventor of chloroform." There is Sir Douglas Mac-lagan, courtly of manner, with a roll of music in his hand; a somewhat Orchardson figure at the piano, singing, most exqui-sitely, the long-forgotten airs out of Italian Opera. And there is one who was not, per-haps, actually of the professorial coterie, Dr. Thomas Keith, tall and spare, with stooping shoulders, a sad face and fair, pointed beard: I have heard him called "The man of sorrows." He was our kind and gentle family doctor.

If Dr. Keith had been available—and I must have known that for some reason he was not—I should have no memory of the great Lister to record; for it would certainly have been Dr. Keith's address that I should have given to the cabman. As it was, the address I gave, on that memorable occasion, was No. 9 Charlotte Square.

We ourselves, by that time, had moved into a house in Regent Terrace. Our parents

were away for the day visiting friends across
the Forth, and were not to be home till late
in the evening. But the sun was still high
in the heavens when the great catastrophe
occurred. One of the maids announced the
fact that she had swallowed a pin. Trembling, and in tears, she managed to say,
between little spasmodic gulps, that it was a
bent pin, and that it was sticking in her
throat, not very far down.

I suppose I fancied myself in charge; at
any rate I assumed an authority which seems
to have been accorded. I sent for a cab, and
the maid and I got into it. I still wonder at
my audacity in driving to Professor Lister's
house in Charlotte Square.

We were shown into the dining-room, and
immediately, while we were still standing,
the great surgeon came in. He stood, silently
benign, looking at us, while I made my little
explanatory appeal. I had prepared it, in
my own mind, as we were driving in the cab.
Our maid had said she had swallowed a pin,
a bent pin—and she felt it sticking in her
throat—not very far down; and my father
and mother (I am afraid I said papa and
mamma; people did in those days) were
away for the day, and I did not quite know
what I ought to do, to whom I ought to

come; but they would be back that evening, and I was sure they would call on him themselves—to thank him—the very next day.

I remember the kind, grave face looking down at me as he listened; and without a word he led the way into his consulting-room. I remember the look of the chair, a glorified dentist's chair, in which he placed the trembling girl. I remember standing by— indeed, she had taken a firm grip of me—and watching the surgeon's hands, their leisurely, gentle manipulation of the long, shining instruments; they seemed to grow longer and longer, as the search for that pin proceeded.

Then, at last, he desisted. "I do not think," he said slowly, looking at the girl in the chair, "there is any pin there. I think, if there had been, I should have found it."

He came with us out into the hall, the girl drying her eyes. At the open door—the cab waiting to take us back—he shook hands.

"You may tell Professor and Mrs. Masson," he said, smiling benignly, "that I don't think there is any pin there. You may say, if there had been, I think I should have found it."

That is my childhood memory of the great surgeon, and I have no other; but my mother, writing to one of her family in London a few months after the pin incident, says:

"We had a most interesting paper of Lister's to read in the last number of the *Medical Journal* . . . he sent it to Mr. Masson. . . . It seems to me we may eventually find a mode of preventing disease, as far as it is carried by means of germs, as completely as we prevent pain by chloroform.   He told Mr. M. *wonderful* things about Carbolic Acid. . . ."

A good many years later I was to know his spray, the "Lister Spray," very well indeed.   Unforgettable, the operating theatre of the great hospital on the Thames Embankment, looking across to the Houses of Parliament.   Unforgettable, the scene—often, even in the daytime, by gaslight; the "Case" for operation, the small group about the table, a human life under an anæsthetic, the raised tiers of students, the tense silence, the faint odour of the carbolised steam, the sense of security in the little hissing whisper of the Lister Spray—the "unconscious care-taker," Lister himself has called it.   It was always there, always whispering.   His little spray, gradually perfected, in use all over the world.

But there came a day—after another interval of years—when, revisiting the old place, and passing along the outside corridor on to which the windows of those operating theatres opened, I stopped suddenly. For I missed something. There was a sense of loss—in the silence. The spray was not whispering.

"I miss the sound of——" I began, and quickly the answer came, "Everything is aseptic, not antiseptic, now."

For a moment the words seemed to me charged with the basest ingratitude; and then the thought came, what must Lister himself be feeling? Sadness, no doubt; the sadness of the teacher, inevitable. Humility; the humility of the student, characteristic. A keen interest, assuredly, in each step forward in the advance of knowledge, even if it meant for him the abandonment of beliefs.

Step by step the march has gone on a great way since Lord Lister died.

We were living in Regent Terrace when Carlyle came to stay with us; an older, sadder, rather tremulous Carlyle, very gentle and tender, still perfervidly brilliant in talk.

He was complaining of sleeplessness, and was much troubled by the noise of the railway whistles, as the North British trains dived into the tunnel outside the Waverley Station. My mother had given him a room on the drawing-room floor at the back of the house, looking out on the tall trees and the Terrace gardens that slope upwards along the Calton Hill. She hoped it was a quiet room. But he heard the whistles; she could not shut out the sound. There was a room at the top of the house that had no window—only a sky-light; and this was offered to Carlyle as possibly a quieter room. He went upstairs with my mother to inspect it, and seemed pleased with it. Then suddenly—down through the sky-light it seemed—came the sound of a long, shrill whistle, and the shriek and rattle of shunting trains. Carlyle laughed, a laugh of grim appreciation, and they went downstairs again.

He was accustomed to have a little tray by his bedside, with a cup of arrowroot on it and biscuits and what not, in case he should lie long awake. And he was very particular that it must be "Bermuda arrow-root." My mother had some difficulty in procuring arrowroot certified as coming from Bermuda, but I think she succeeded; and each night the little tray went up, holding a most astonishing variety of small quantities of good things; and each morning it came down again with all the things on it— Bermuda arrowroot and all—untouched. My mother comforted herself by thinking that perhaps, after all, Carlyle did know something of the "sleep that knits up the ravell'd sleeve of care."

"DEAR MASSON," he wrote after he had left us. "This morning I find (a sharp shower reminding me) that the indispensable *mackintosh* is still hanging amid its kindred miscellanea in yr Hall! Brown paper parcel (unpaid) by the Caledon[n]. railway: that is the clear remedy; one other bit of trouble I had still to add to the big kindness already accumulated *there*. Nothing else of harm was in the journey yest[y].; which I happily got transacted, after Abington Station, in perfect solitude, in mute dialogue with the misty mountains and *their* sad and great unfathomable preachings and prophesyings to me. Brother and nephew were in waiting at the poor *advent*; here I have since had five or six hours of sound deep sleep, and already feel to be approaching the old mark ag[n].

"Of one thing I have, and shall retain, a right glad and thankful memory, the warmly human way in wh[h]. you all rec[d]. me and wrapt my infirmities and me in soft down, in sympathy & ministrat^n. of your best. Not even the railway whistles and other *infernalia* of the case deprive me of that or indeed do other than enhance all that.

"But my journey, I find, was radically wrong-schemed. It was of the nature of a relig^s. *Pilgrimage* (truly such to me, in this now wholly irrelig^s. world). I should have made direct for Hadd^n. and back, communicat^g. with no mortal; then would there have been nothing that was not sacred that was *not* sacred, that was mundane, basely miserable and profane. As it is, the hour I had in the Abbey Kirk, that half-hour interview with noble old Betty, and the gen^l. element thro'out in Regent Terrace, these do remain to me like jewels set in—I will not say what.

"Thanks and kindest regards to you all, ye friendly ministering souls. . . .—Yours ever,

T. CARLYLE."

Another summer—it cannot have been long after this visit—Carlyle came unexpectedly to see us at Leven. Our parents were at home in Regent Terrace, and I had been sent down, in so-called charge of the younger members of the family, to a tiny cottage near the Leven links, where we were living in a state of perpetual picnic. Carlyle and his niece, Mary Aitken (afterwards Mrs. Alexander Carlyle), were staying with Provost Swan at Kirkcaldy, and Carlyle had expressed a wish to call on "Masson's children." Accordingly, one morning at a midway hour between breakfast and luncheon, we saw, to our consternation, an enormous wagonette and pair of horses draw up outside the rustic porch of Woodbine Cottage; and Carlyle, with Mary Aitken and Provost Swan, descended upon us. They completely filled our little parlour.

I cannot remember what we talked about, but I do remember that Carlyle with a wave of his hand peremptorily refused—for himself, and also for Mary Aitken and Provost Swan—my rather timid offer of late breakfast or early lunch. And presently he said he thought of leaving the wagonette and setting out by himself along the shore to "have a bathe in the sea." Mary Aitken, in her wise and quiet way, demurred; and Carlyle turned to me rather sadly, and said he was beginning to feel he ought to be tied with a bit of string to Mary's hand, so that she could always keep him from going too far away from her. But he did have his bathe in the sea.

A happier picture of Carlyle in the 'seventies, and quite as characteristic, is given in a letter of my father's, written from the Athenæum Club in London, to my mother at home. He had been to see Carlyle in Chelsea.

"We had a smoke and chat in his house, Miss Aitken dropping in; and then we had a long walk through Kensington Gardens and Hyde Park. We sat for a little while under a tree, and he was very confidential—answering my question whether it was true he had been offered a Baronetcy by saying it was quite true, and done very handsomely by Disraeli. . . . At parting, near the Marble Arch, he found he had left the red handkerchief which he had spread to sit on, under the tree in Kensington Gardens; and I believe he went back by the same route through the gardens, bent on finding the handkerchief if it was still there."

One other recollection of Carlyle I have, and it is my last; the last time I ever saw him.

My mother and I were in London together; and this is a part of her letter to my father at home:

"Yesterday, F—— and I went to Chelsea . . ., and spent an hour with Carlyle. He looked a perfect picture of a golden old age, in a grey gown, in his beautiful drawing-room,

among the well-arranged antiquities and
pictures and with the rose of health on his
dear old face. He was as kind as possible,
talked splendidly about Sir Th. More, Eras-
mus, Luther, the Elector Frederick of Saxony
—his successors—Frederick the Great—his
sister—Cromwell and Milton. He showed us,
as the texts of his discourse, the pictures on
the walls, and kept us after we proposed to
go. He often said 'but Masson says so and
so,' or 'Masson tells me such and such a
thing,' showing how amusing he has found
your conversation. . . . When we said good-
bye he kissed us both twice over—lifting up
our veils—and his dear face quivered a little
as if he thought we might not meet again.
He came down to the door with us, and
showed us other pictures in the dining-room;
and his last words were 'God bless you—and
all good be with you!' It was a rare pleasure
for us both, I assure you."

During one of our visits to London, somewhere in the 'seventies, we spent an evening
with the Forbes-Robertsons. My mother
and father had called, taking me with them,
to say good-bye before returning to Edinburgh next day. They were dear old friends,
and their eldest son (afterwards Sir Johnston
Forbes-Robertson) was my father's godson.
At that time Johnston Forbes-Robertson was
acting in the *Lady of Lyons*, I think at the

Prince of Wales's Theatre, with Ellen Terry, and we had been, some nights before, to see the play. Though it is so long ago the grace and dignity of their acting throughout remains in my memory, especially in the scene where they came out from the French window into the moonlight of the garden, and the very young actor's wonderful voice, as he wrapped his black travelling-cloak about the beautiful woman in white satin—"One cloak shall cover both!"

On the evening when we called to say good-bye his mother, Mrs Forbes-Robertson, asked us to stay to supper. Ellen Terry was coming in after the play was over, and if we waited we should see her too. We were already in the supper-room when the door opened and she came in, followed by Johnston Forbes-Robertson. She was still wearing the white satin and pearls of the last scene. Very lovely she looked, and very animated was her talk and manner at the supper-table. I think she must have noticed my gaze of wondering admiration—I was sitting opposite to her—for suddenly she sprang up, came round behind her hostess's chair, and knelt down by me. Putting up her hands and making a cup of them to hold her beautiful and clever face, she looked up at me.

"This is to show you," she said, with some feeling, "that it is *not real*. It is all false!—all false!"

She touched the pearls about her throat; and then, without giving time for any response, sprang up again, took her place by Mrs. Forbes-Robertson, and resumed her animated talk with others at the table.

Often as I saw her afterwards in her many great parts, I have never felt that any of them was so really real as the Ellen Terry that she herself had called "not real" of that evening in the 'seventies.

As for the eldest son of the house, then at the outset of his brilliant career—with him and Lady Forbes-Robertson, and even to the third generation—the old friendship continues to this day.

CHAPTER IX

MAINLY ABOUT STEVENSON AND BROWNING

PROFESSOR AND MRS. FLEEMING JENKIN, who
had come to Edinburgh in 1868, were a great
addition to the University coterie. He, like
my father, was an importation from London
University College. He was a man of extraordinary vigour and thoroughness in everything he did, and with many tastes outside
his own scientific work—work that had
earned for him the title of "medical attendant
to the Atlantic Cable." Mrs. Jenkin—something of *grande dame,* and reputed to be a
Greek scholar, educated by her scholarly
father—proved from the very beginning a
delightful hostess. She not only brought
with her literary tastes and associations, but
she was one of the most finished house-
managers I ever knew. Everything went
like clockwork—and you scarcely heard its
ticking. "Madam," her family called her;
and yet, I remember how simply she told my
mother about her Surrey cottage and the
beehives, with the honey in them, that she

was so sorry to leave behind. She and my mother became good friends; and though she had no daughter of her own, she was very kind to me.

My first recollection of Louis Stevenson is a hazy one, dating back to a bitterly cold winter in the early 'seventies, when all Edinburgh was skating on Duddingston Loch. My brother and I were skating there one day, more or less with the Fleeming Jenkins; but Professor and Mrs. Jenkin almost always skated together on a little well-swept oval of ice which seemed to have become their special property. Mrs. Jenkin, easily tired, used to kneel in the centre of this, looking, in her close-fitting winter garb, the outline of profile against the white banks and jagged, frozen reeds, the hands held in front of her in the small muff, rather like an effigy against the wall of an old church. And the Professor described wonderful figures round about his kneeling wife, circling and pirouetting by himself till she seemed to be rested, when they took hands again. Louis Stevenson came and went about them, skating alone; a slender, dark figure with a muffler about his neck; darting in and out among the crowd, and disappearing and reappearing like a melancholy minnow among the tall reeds that fringe the Loch.   I remember that we walked home, several of us together—but not Professor and Mrs. Jenkin—by the Queen's Park and Arthur Seat, all white with snow.   And Louis Stevenson came part of the way with us, walking a little separately from us—it was a case, with us all, of heads down against a biting north-east wind—and then turned off by himself across the snow, somewhere about St. Leonards, towards the Old Town.

My next recollection is a much more vivid one, of a dinner-party at the house of Louis Stevenson's parents, in Heriot Row; one of the "young dinners" that were rather prevalent in Edinburgh at that time.   It was a pleasant little dinner of twelve or fourteen. One or two sisters and brothers had come together; all were young members of Edinburgh families, and some were more or less intimates in the house in Heriot Row.   It was my first visit there, and the first grown-up dinner-party at which I can remember being present.

Diagonally opposite, across the flowers and silver of the dinner-table, I could see Sir Walter Simpson on Mrs. Stevenson's right hand; and I have still in my memory the picture of the pretty mother, at the head of her table, gently vivacious; and of the young

Sir Walter, somewhat languidly attentive to her all dinner-time.

Our end of the table was, to me, almost uncomfortably brilliant. Mr. Stevenson had taken me in, and Louis Stevenson was on my other side. Father and son both talked, taking diametrically opposite points of view on all things under the sun. Mr. Stevenson seemed to me, on that evening, to be the type of the kindly, orthodox Edinburgh father. We chatted of nice, concrete, comfortable things, such as the Scottish Highlands in autumn; and in a moment of Scottish fervour he quoted—I believe *sotto voce*—a bit of a versified psalm. But Louis Stevenson, on my other side, was that evening in one of his most recklessly brilliant moods. His talk was almost incessant. I felt quite dazed at the amount of intellection he expended on each subject, however trivial in itself, that we touched upon. He worried it as a dog might worry a rat, and then threw it off lightly, as some chance word or allusion set him thinking, and talking, of something else. The father's face at certain moments was a study; an indescribable mixture of vexation, fatherly pride and admiration, and sheer bewilderment at his son's brilliant flippancies and the quick young thrusts of his wit and criticism.

Our talk turned on realism as a duty of the novelist. Louis Stevenson had been reading Balzac. He was fascinated by Balzac; steeped in Balzac. It was as if he had left Balzac and all his books locked up in some room upstairs—had turned the key on him, with a "Stay there, my dear fellow, and I'll come back as soon as I can get away from this dinner!"

I knew nothing about Balzac, and I believe I said so. I remember feeling sorry and rather ashamed that I did not know; and Louis Stevenson began telling me about Balzac, and about his style and vocabulary; and I felt grateful to the father for at least appearing to know as little about Balzac as I did, and to care even less. It may have been Balzac's vocabulary that set us talking about the English language; the father and son debated, with some heat, the subject of word-coinage and the use of modern slang. Mr. Stevenson upheld the doctrine of a "well of English undefiled," which of course made Louis Stevenson rattle off with extraordinary ingenuity whole sentences composed of words of foreign origin taken into our language from all parts of the world—words of the East, of classical Europe, of the West Indies, and modern American slang. By a string of sentences he proved the absurdity of such a doctrine, and indeed its practical impossibility. It was a real feat in the handling of language, and I can see to this day his look of pale triumph. The father was silenced; but for a moment he had been almost tearfully in earnest. One could see it was not a matter of mere vocabulary with him.

Everybody now knows how strongly attached, for all their antagonisms of temperament, the father and son were to one another; but on the evening of this little dinner-party we were all living "at least in this thy day." We have Louis Stevenson's own word for it : "Since I have been away," he wrote, long afterwards, "I have found out for the first time how I love that man."

In the drawing-room upstairs, after dinner, there was a change in the atmospheric conditions. I sat with Mrs. Stevenson on a sofa on one side of the fire, and when the men came in there was no more argument, nor, indeed, any brilliant talk. Louis Stevenson stood, facing us, listening to the talk and laughter of others, a slight, boyish figure with a very pale face and luminous eyes, one of a little group of men in the centre of the room. And certainly on that occasion Louis Stevenson wore ordinary conventional evening dress, "but not exprest in fancy."

Mr. Charles Baxter brought a small chair and sat down on it in front of the sofa where Mrs. Stevenson and I were sitting; and, tilting the chair backwards, he broke off a piece of the wood, and instead of seeming sorry or apologetic, handed it with mock gravity to Mrs. Stevenson: "My dear Mrs. Stevenson," he said, "this is what comes of having cheap furniture!"

Louis Stevenson, from where he stood, watched this performance, but took no notice of it; and Mrs. Stevenson, with a glance round her drawing-room, laughed a contented little laugh and laid the offending bit of walnut wood on the arm of the sofa beside her.

As everybody knows, Louis Stevenson was only intermittently in Edinburgh, with its "icy winds and conventions," during the years that followed. I believe he owed many of his lightest-hearted hours to the friendship of Professor and Mrs. Jenkin. Certainly it is impossible to recall the Louis Stevenson of the 'seventies except as one—a favoured one—of the delightful Jenkin coterie.

What a feature in our Edinburgh winters

were those dear old "private theatricals,"
to which we were so hospitably invited, in
Professor and Mrs. Jenkin's own house! The
wall between the dining-room and the room
behind it had been made to "let down" in
some mysterious way, to form a stage, with
a real curtain and footlights; and night
after night the audiences were packed into
the dining-room. Each successive winter,
there was the same pleasant secrecy as to
"what it was going to be this year"; if
it were to be "something of Shakespeare's,"
or "from the Greek," or "something new."
The members of the little company were
always very loyal in keeping up the mystery
to the last possible moment, and then, when
it leaked out, there was always the important
question, "Which night are you asked for?"
And afterwards there were all sorts of com-
ments and criticisms, and the theatricals
continued to be talked about till a fresh fall
of snow heralded the approach of our Edinburgh summer. With all this, I fear we
were not always grateful enough for the
immense amount of trouble that was taken
to teach us what dramatic art might be
under the domestic roof.

Louis Stevenson was not one of the chief
actors in that company. Yet there are

people who remember his Orsino in *Twelfth Night*—the slender figure in the "splendid Francis I. clothes, heavy with gold and stage jewellery" and the satisfied languor of his opening words:

> " If Music be the food of love, play on.
>   Give me excess of it, that, surfeiting,
>   The appetite may sicken, and so die.
>   That strain again! it had a dying fall."

But it was not so much the play that Louis Stevenson enjoyed, nor even the "thrill of admiration" in successive audiences, as to "sup afterwards with those clothes on," amid all the Shakespearian wit and raillery and badinage that circulated about the supper-table: "That," he wrote, "is something to live for."

I have some humorous recollections of Louis Stevenson in the green-room. On one occasion I saw him walking up and down a little bit of the big drawing-room, looking, in a dreamy, detached way each time he passed, into a mirror that was hung on the line of sight. It was as if he were acting to himself being an actor; and then he brought carmine and powder, and began making himself up, peering gravely close into the little glass.

Another time he fell to disputing with a

bigger and altogether more muscular member
of the company as to which of the two could
claim to have *the larger girth of calf.* Louis
Stevenson was under the impression his own
was the larger; and so in earnest was he,
and so anxious to prove his case, that he
actually fetched—an inch-tape, and inveigled
his muscular friend into kneeling on the
drawing-room carpet, while each, with much
solemnity, measured the other's calf!

But once Louis Stevenson surpassed himself. It was in Greek tragedy. The curtain
had fallen on a powerful and moving scene,
amid the applause of the audience, and the
stage was left in the possession of two of the
young actors—Mr. Hole and my brother—both
in Greek garb. In a momentary reaction
after so much unrelieved tragedy, these two,
oblivious of their classic draperies, threw
themselves into one another's arms, per-
formed a rapid war-dance, and then flung
themselves on to opposite ends of a couch
at the back of the stage, with their feet
meeting in a kind of triumphal arch in the
centre. Louis Stevenson, who had been
officiating at the curtain, took one look at
them. He touched a spring, and up went the
curtain again.

The audience, scarcely recovered from the

tragic scene on which the curtain had fallen, gave one gasp of amazement, and then broke into a roar of applause. That roar was the first thing that showed the two luckless acrobats that something had happened. They leapt to their feet, only to see the curtain fall once more. Professor Jenkin, who was host and stage-manager in one, had been watching this particular portion of the play from the front. Without a word, he left his seat and went behind the scenes. "Mr. Stevenson," he said, with icy distinctness, "I shall ask you to give me a few minutes in my own room."

Anybody who ever saw Louis Stevenson can imagine the little enigmatic flutter of a smile, the deprecatory bend of the head, with which he followed the Professor. What happened in that stage-manager's room? There was some trepidation among the members of the company; and a furtive whisper circulated among them: "*Can it be corporal punishment?*" And there was a general feeling of relief when Louis Stevenson sauntered into the drawing-room with a look of absolute unconcern.

But one of the little company—the brilliant, charming, irrepressible Leila Scot-Skirving (afterwards Mrs Maturin), had been interested enough to linger behind the others, and to waylay Louis Stevenson as he left the Professor's room. I am indebted to her brother, Archie Scot-Skirving, for the end of this anecdote.

"What happened?" she whispered; and Louis whispered back: "The very worst ten minutes I ever experienced in the whole course of my life!"

In March 1878 there was a big bazaar in the Music Hall in Edinburgh, to raise a sum of money for a University Cricket Field. Professor Jenkin and Mr. Ewing (afterwards Sir Alfred Ewing, and Vice-Chancellor of Edinburgh University) had been reading in *The Times* a paragraph describing Edison's invention, and, as "something fell to be done for a University Cricket Ground Bazaar," as R. L. S. has expressed it, the idea occurred to them to have a phonograph made in Edinburgh by the firm of gas-engineers who used to do experimental work for them, and to exhibit it at the bazaar. It was a memorable moment when the instrument was brought finished to Mr. Ewing, and he first heard the magic small voice. Louis Stevenson has called this phonograph "a toy that touched the skirts of life, art and science, a toy prolific of problems and theories"; and indeed as soon as Professor Jenkin and Mr. Ewing heard it articulate they began to use it for their own scientific work. Meantime, it was the great feature of the bazaar.

Two phonographs had been made, one of which was raffled. Sir William Thomson (Lord Kelvin) was extremely anxious to obtain it, and bought a great many raffle-tickets—and he won it. In a room off the gallery in the Music Hall (admission one shilling) Professor Jenkin and Mr. Ewing took turns to give "lecturettes," with experiments, on the phonograph. "It is the realisation"—so runs the little old handbill— "of Baron Munchausen's horn, only more so." In another room (admission half a crown) Mrs. Jenkin presided, exhibiting the other phonograph to visitors, who were allowed to speak to it and hear the repetition of their own voices; and she herself spoke to it a *répertoire* of previously rehearsed sentences which had been found specially successful for the purpose. Among these, I remember, were Hamlet's "What's Hecuba to him, or he to Hecuba?" which the little voice repeated with dutiful precision; and the phrase of the moment, the British sentiment which had caught on : "We don't want to fight, but by Jingo if we do!" which gave away the phonograph completely as a militarist of the deepest dye.

Some of us were there, giving assistance of the "Walk up, ladies and gentlemen!" order; and my recollection is that Louis Stevenson came and went, watching the performance with an amused smile, more interested in the human by-play than in the science of the toy. By his own account, he and Mr. Hole treated the phonograph "with unscientific laughter, commemorating various shades of Scottish accent, or proposing to 'teach the poor dumb animal to swear.'"

In that room off the gallery in the Music Hall there was plenty of by-play to amuse us all. I remember two ladies, apparently sisters, stately and demure, dressed alike in black spangled with sequins, who listened earnestly to Mrs. Jenkin's mellifluous "What's Hecuba to him, or he to Hecuba?"

"Ah, what indeed!" said one of the sisters softly; and the other murmured: "There seems to be no immediate response!"

A burly, farmer-looking man threw down his half-crown and made for the instrument —and then stepped back, overcome by a sudden shyness. Mrs. Jenkin hastened to the rescue, with the unfailing question about Hecuba; but it was evident that to him, at

any rate, Hecuba was nothing. He scorned
Hecuba. The Jingo sentiment was more to
his taste; but he wanted to speak for himself and to hear his own voice speak back to
him. Once he made a nervous plunge,
pulling up his cuffs as if he were going to
fight the phonograph. At last he bellowed
into it, with a mighty voice: "What a
wonderrrful instrrrument y'arrre!"

And back came the small Puckish voice,
delightedly—

"What a wonderrrful instrrrument y'arrre!'

The burly man flushed, and paled. "It's
no canny!" he muttered, and fled.

It was a good many years after all this had
happened that one day, early in summer, I
was walking with Leila Maturin in Princes
Street. There had, in these years, been
great changes in Edinburgh. For some time,
of course, nothing had been seen of Louis
Stevenson. The brilliant Jenkin coterie, of
which he had been one of the most brilliant
members, was broken up, dissolved. The
survivors of the little company had gone on
their various ways; I too had been away from
Edinburgh. All had found their work in a
busy world. Louis Stevenson's father, the
dear old Scotsman with his fervours and his
prejudices, had just been laid to his rest.

An open cab, with a man and woman in it, seated side by side and leaning back—the rest of the cab piled high with rather untidy luggage—came slowly towards us, westward, along Princes Street. It was evidently carrying travellers to the railway station. As it passed us slowly, out on the broad roadway (for Princes Street in the 'eighties was not what it is to-day), a slender, loose-garbed figure stood up in the ·cab and waved a wide-brimmed hat.

"Good-bye!" he called to us—"Good-bye!"

"It is Louis Stevenson!" said Leila Maturin. "He must be going away again!"

Was this the Louis Stevenson of the 'seventies, the boy who had played truant from the college classes; the "queer, lank lad in a velvet coat," whose unhappy face and brilliant talk had so perplexed and charmed us?

The cab passed. The grey vista of our Northern Capital, the long line of Princes Street, was at its very best as Louis Stevenson looked back at it and us, over the back of the open cab, still waving his hat and calling "Good-bye!" That little bit of west-endy, east-windy Edinburgh, with the grey and green of the Castle rock and the gardens on the one side, and Princes Street itself, glittering in the sunshine, on the other! It was Edinburgh's last sight of Louis Stevenson, and Louis Stevenson's last look back at the city that was his birthplace, in which he had been so happy and so miserable; that he had chafed against and railed at; that he was to write about and dream about, in exile, and to love immeasurably to the end.

As far back as 1879, the year after the Phonograph Bazaar for the University Cricket Field, Sir Alexander Grant and the Senatus had begun to make preparations for the University Tercentenary. My recollection is that the April of 1884 was unusually genial—for our climate. There is among our relics of the time a list of the cabs ordered by our mother—in good time beforehand—to take our guests and us to and from the various functions that filled those four crowded days of Festival. It is an alarming list; and here and there in it, against a particular cab, or brace of cabs, is a rather pathetic little note: "Open, if the day is fine." But there was one cab that does not appear in the list.

Our brother Orme (Sir David Orme Masson) was one of the three joint Presidents of the

first Students' Representative Council of
Edinburgh University, and on him fell much
of the responsibility of the Council's activities
during those four days and nights. I think
that cab was what would now be called a
whole-time cab, for it was chartered for the
period of the Festival, to come and go between our house (we were then in Great King
Street), the University, the Theatre Royal,
the U.P. Synod Hall, the Music Hall and
Assembly Rooms, and the *Scotsman* office.
I can hear now the patient pawing of the
horse's hoof on the rough stones in front of
our door, in the darkness of night and in the
pale grey of the April dawn.

And what can I remember of the Festival
itself?

Our own guests—personal friends—were
the Count and Countess Saffi and Robert
Browning. The Saffis came from Bologna,
he as Delegate from that University, where
he was Professor of the History of Public
Law; but in 1849 he had been, with Mazzini
and Armellini, one of the Triumvirate of
Rome; and he retained a certain sad state-
liness of manner. His charming Scottish
wife, who had been before her marriage
Georgina Craufurd, was the daughter of one
of the most important of the "Friends of

Italy" in the political London of the 'fifties. She was now as Italian as the Count himself, who indeed spoke very beautiful English. Both were old friends of our parents.

Robert Browning was the Prince of Guests, always appreciative and interested; quietly genial, whether in his scarlet robes of the Oxford D.C.L., or in his navy-blue short coat that he wore when he came down, dark-eyed and with a very damp white head, to breakfast; or in evening dress, with his crush-hat, a fascinating disc, under his arm.

My father had known Browning for some years. The following is the continuation of my father's letter which I have already quoted, about his walk with Carlyle in Kensington Gardens:—

. . . "The previous evening I had dined at Sir Henry Thompson's. There were nine there—the host, Browning, Herbert Spencer, Charlton Bastian, Sir Frederick Pollock (editor of *Macready's Memoirs*), Greenwood (editor of *Pall Mall*), Knowles (editor of *Contemporary*), W. K. Clifford, and myself. He calls these little dinners 'my octaves' . . . all very neat and artistic—lamps subdued, etc. No ladies present. We had a cigarette at the dinner-table and then adjourned to a kind of sanctuary downstairs— hung round with paintings by the host himself and others, and with cabinets of precious old blue crockery—for further chat and smoking. Before dinner, while we were waiting, Browning reminded me of our old acquaintance, and drew me to the window as if he wanted to tell me something. Nearly opposite, in Wimpole Street, is No. 50, and he pointed out that house to me as the house in which his wife had lived from her infancy (it belonged to her father) and written most of her poems. After dinner, I had a good deal of more talk with him—more than ever before—and found him very clever, and very full of apt anecdote, with plenty of humour, and a frequent touch of sarcasm. I will remember some of his stories to tell you: especially two or three about *coincidences*. Remind me. . . ."

The evening before the Tercentenary Ceremonial, there was a little dress-rehearsal in our drawing-room. Madame Saffi came in, bringing with her the Count in the beautiful robes of his Bologna University, in which he was to appear next morning. He was made to stand in the middle of the room, under the lights, as she displayed him to us— looking stately, indeed; gravely amused; a little deprecatory. Browning watched for a minute or two, then slipped out of the room, and came back putting on his own scarlet gown of the Oxford D.C.L. "I have a gown too!" he said lightly, showing himself off.

Of all the happenings of those four days the most memorable to me was the Reception given by the Students of the University, with Sir Stafford Northcote, as Lord Rector, in the Chair. It was addressed by several of the Delegates; among them Russell Lowell, the American Minister; Count Saffi, speaking in English; de Lesseps, speaking in French; Virchow, speaking in German; Pasteur, von Helmholtz, Lord Reay. A brilliant selection of speakers; but, above them all, I remember Virchow, and the words in which he warned the eager young students of Science in our University against the danger of following mere logical possibilities: "*logische Möglichkeiten.*"

At the end the whole great meeting rose with cries of "Browning! Browning!" And Browning—who had extracted a promise that he should not be asked to speak—stood up, and then and there made the first and only speech of his life.

CHAPTER X

FLORENCE NIGHTINGALE AND LATER FRIENDSHIPS

It was strange to be living again in London; and not the London of one's childhood nor of pleasant visits, but a south-east London, in close proximity to Nine Elms and Doulton's Works, and Westminster Bridge Road. From a balcony, high over the Thames, one looked across the great river at the Houses of Parliament and the long line of the Victoria Embankment. The chimes of Big Ben marked off inexorably every fifteen minutes of the days and nights.

Wordsworth's statement about "that mighty Heart" did not apply to Westminster Bridge in the 'eighties. The throb and murmur—the "roar of London"—was always heard, except perhaps for about three-quarters of an hour in the very early dawn; and after that the sound of the market-garden carts began, heavy and honest, coming in from the South on their way to Covent Garden; and sometimes the pathetic rustle and hurry and patter of little sheep, also coming in from the South on their way, probably, to Smithfield.

Westminster Bridge itself seemed to span two different worlds. One summer in the hot and excitable 'eighties, it was reported that the politicians and their friends, having tea on the Terrace, had complained of the unsightliness of scarlet jackets and blue and white quilts on the balconies of St Thomas's Hospital, opposite. And Sir William Mac-Cormac, the great surgeon, hearing this, had retorted, in a flash, "Tell them, their own Parliamentary proceedings have lost every vestige of decency!"

But the broad river itself was the Mediator. Who that has ever lived actually on its banks —on either of its banks—can forget the moving panorama of sights and sounds; the shunting, the whistling, the slip of chains; the faint hoarse cries; the distant church clocks; the little scarlet-funnelled penny steamers that zigzagged from one landing-stage to another; the barges of "black diamonds" that puffed and snorted importantly, sending up a friendly shriek as they passed, a signal of greeting—not to any Member of Parliament, but to some sick bargee-mate, who was sure to be looking down wistfully from one of those hospital balconies. And among them all, slowly, almost imperceptibly, the majestic hay-barges moved down mid-stream, bringing with them the scent of the hayfields, as they carried their high-piled freight into the Pool of London.

" Above all ryuers the Ryuer hath renowne
   Whose beryall stremys pleasant and preclare
   Under thy lusty wallys renneth downe,
   Where many a swanne doth swimme with wingis fare,
   Where many a ship doth rest with toppe-royall :
   O ! towne of townes, patrone and not compare ;
   London, thou art the Flour of cities all."

Not the first Scotsman, old Dunbar, nor yet the last, to look passionately London-wards.

My father had known Canon Ainger since the early days of *Macmillan's Magazine*, in which—in the December number, 1859—there had appeared the article "Books and their Uses" over the signature "Doubleday" (A.A.). Perhaps it was this old association that made Canon Ainger, soon after I began working in London, send me a little sheaf of his visiting-cards, to give admission to the Temple services, "with the Reader of the Temple's kind regards."

Those were the days when Vaughan was Master and Ainger Reader of the Temple, and Dr. Hopkins was at the organ. Canon Ainger's reputation as a reader and a preacher was then drawing strangers from all parts of the world. There was a peculiar charm in the Temple services; the special character of the congregation; rows of strong legal heads in the centre of the church; the hereditary Service Books of the Benchers; the "Bidding Prayer"; the beautiful voices of the choir; the historic, mellow old organ. Not the least charm was the personality of the Reader himself, whom some people will still remember. "Writer, Humourist, Divine," he has been called; a slightly stooping figure, a meditative face, a very white head gently moving to the rhythm of the music he so loved. His reading of the service was perfect; his sermon, carefully written, full of shy, human sympathy, was cameo-cut; a fragment of pure literature.

It was such a sermon that he preached one very hot Sunday afternoon, when I found myself in the Temple Church. In dreams I had been beholding the Hebrides; for my people were going, as usual, to the Highlands, and it would be the first autumn holiday for many a long day that I had not shared with them. Only after the service began did I realise that it was the very last Sunday in Term; that the Courts were rising, the Temple was closing. Everybody was going out of town. "A Holiday Sermon."

And the text !—"Make the men sit down. Now there was much grass in the place."

The preacher explained that it was his intention to speak, not to those who were going on holiday, but to those whose work obliged them to remain in town.

I cannot after all these years venture to quote from Canon Ainger's sermon, which pointed out the green freshness of many things hidden away all round us in the heat and dust of a city life. When the congregation came out into Fleet Street, the little old shop windows, those humble eating-houses, with lobster-claws spread on lettuce leaves, and pale yellow lemons stuck in the necks of glass bottles, took on another aspect. The odours of soups and wines and cheap cigars seemed no longer wholly un-pleasant. "Much grass in the place." Surely, that little bit of London round about the Inns of Court and the old Temple Church was full of it. I remember sending home for Cunningham's *London*, *Pepys's Diary*, *Evelyn's Diary*, the *Essays of Elia*, and the *Annals of Our Time*. And I found

my grass, that autumn, in a world of hot
pavements, hoarse street-cries, the stream
and pressure of omnibuses, and the continual
calling of "Benk!—one penny!" and "Elephant! Elephant!—penny *all* the way!"

Long afterwards, when Canon Ainger was
Master of the Temple, and was lying ill
there, in the Master's House — not long
before he died—I wrote to him, from Edinburgh, to tell him how gratefully I had
always remembered that Holiday Sermon
of the 'eighties. And his answer came at
once, saying that he had been ill and was
lying there, and telling me also of a little
coincidence. To occupy himself, he had
asked for a packet of his old sermons to be
brought to him. He had been looking
through them, and had come upon that
Holiday Sermon, with the text "Now there
was much grass in the place." He had
been reading it just before my letter arrived.

I think it was in 1887 that I came to
know Miss Nightingale. Many a visit have
I paid her in the house in South Street, Park
Lane—the street of Georgian houses, now
pulled down — so near to Hyde Park and
Piccadilly, and yet so quaint and retired;
full of memories of more or less celebrated

men and women, who lived and loved and died there.

I can hear now the pleasant clop-clop and jingle of the hansom that brought me there, and set me down, punctual to the minute, at the door of No. 10; jingling away again almost before the door was opened. My visits were always of a pattern, and always by appointment; and they were scattered over a whole decade of life. They had a quaint beginning.

One day I saw a commissionaire, resplendent with ribands and medals on his coat, coming towards me along the open corridor of St. Thomas's Hospital.

"With Miss Florence Nightingale's compliments," he said, and put into my hands a basket of eggs.

There must have been a note or message with the eggs in the basket. I know I wrote thanking Miss Nightingale; and soon afterwards, by invitation, I paid my first visit to the house in South Street, where the invalided "Chief" was spending the sunset years of her world-famous life.

The great Crimean episode was long over. The years that had followed it, the pioneer work of the organiser and "passionate statistician," were now also drawing to a close.

The pioneer was beginning to see her own reforms running ahead of her desires and beliefs. At seventy, with still twenty years of life before her, she lay on her couch, gently majestic in her soft invalidism; still intense in her devotion to everything that concerned what had been her life's work.

There was a little sitting-room on the ground floor, in which, on arrival, the visitor waited—a depressing little room, evidently not lived in. There were prints on the walls —portraits, if I remember rightly, of Sidney Herbert and Lord Raglan; and there was one bright little water-colour drawing, hung rather low, of crimsoning American creeper festooning a window in one of the Nightingale country homes. But the clock on the mantelpiece had stopped. In all my visits I never saw the hands of that clock moving. It had irrevocably stopped.

Then the maid came and took the visitor upstairs to Miss Nightingale's room—a light, airy, curtainless room, the general effect one of whiteness, simplicity, flowers. The windows opened on to a balcony, where sometimes the sparrows were pecking at breadcrumbs.

The Chief, in a soft black gown, lay on her couch, leaning back against her cushions.

The satin quilt of military scarlet gave a touch of vivid colour, and she wore a white lace shawl over her smoothly parted hair, and more than one shawl, of white lace, or fine white Shetland wool, over her ample shoulders. A pencil and notebook lay by her hand; and a table at her side held pamphlets, a blue-book, and the tall glass of barley-water set there by the maid who brought the visitor's little tea-table and tea-tray. The visitor's chair, an old-fashioned, little chintz-covered easy-chair, with rather sagging springs, was placed always in exactly the same position, at the side of Miss Nightingale's couch.

I have many memories of those visits. She spoke of many things. She very seldom —only once or twice, I think, in all those years—spoke to me of incidents or persons connected with the Crimean War; but then it was with intense feeling, almost in a whisper. More often she was interested in things going on at the moment, things of which she approved or disapproved—with a glint of mischief in her eyes, or with a ring of vehemence in her voice. Always the statistician, she would put questions; and it was rather disturbing to see the pencil and notebook come into use, and one's answers carefully written down. She liked to be talked to; to be told things. Once I remember telling her a story that had been handed down in our family, of a little dinner at the Chadwicks' house at Richmond, in the early days of the Crimean War. Carlyle and his wife and my parents were the guests, and after dinner Mrs. Carlyle lay on a sofa and described, with all her caustic wit, to my mother and Mrs. Chadwick, a scene between Miss Nightingale and a certain enthusiastic Peeress who had applied to be taken on as one of the little band of Crimean nurses. Miss Nightingale—so the story ran—evidently thinking the applicant quite unsuitable, had become severely matter-of-fact, laying stress on all the hardships and unpleasantnesses, and had ended by saying:

"You would have a weekly allowance of so much for your washing, and a daily allowance of so much for your beer or porter."

Miss Nightingale enjoyed the story; and when I told her I had always wanted to ask her if it were true, she smiled—a mischievous little smile.

"It might be true, my dear. Yes—it might be true."

One late afternoon in summer, the windows on to the balcony were open. Hyde Park—the rolling carriages, the fashion and beauty, the sounds and perfumes of the London season seemed very near to us in that quiet room.

Suddenly Miss Nightingale stopped speaking and held up her hand.

"Listen!" she said.

A weird, faint cry sounded over Hyde Park. I looked at Miss Nightingale, questioning.

"The Hourly Cry to Prayer," she whispered, "from the Mosque."

She explained that a Mohammedan potentate was a guest of that London season.

The sound died away. To the gay, moving throng in the Park below it was inaudible. To me it was strange and startling. But the Lady with the Lamp knew it well. It was to her a reminder of the scenes of her youth's splendid achievement.

There came a day when somehow I felt I should not see her again. To *remember*— even the things and people she had most cared for—seemed to tire her.

"Dear, dear old friend!" she said, more than once; and when I stood up to go and kissed her hand, she assured me "This is not good-bye!"

At the door I looked back. She lay there, a beautiful old picture, against her pillows. She was looking after me, her hands held out in a way she had when you first came in, and

she welcomed you. "Not—not good-bye!"
she repeated.

But it was good-bye.

Our friendship with Sir William and Lady
Ramsay began long before his many honours
came to him, and shortly before their
marriage in 1881. He was my brother's
friend; and he came to stay with us during
an autumn holiday. Before he came we had
been told that he "could do everything, and
do it better than anybody else," and on that
account we were feeling a little afraid of our
expected guest. But we need not have been.
It is true that he was in his element in any
sort of boat—preferably an old sailing-boat
—and that he remained unconcerned when
the latest *Transactions of the Chemical
Society* were brought home soaked in salt
water at the end of a delightful day. He
sketched and he whistled. Many people
must remember his wonderful whistling of
"Should he Upbraid." And when he happened to see a piece of "crewel work"—the
embroidery of the moment—he took it up and
plied his needle as to the manner born.

Sir William Ramsay's students remember
him with gratitude and affection, not only
as a great teacher, but as their personal

friend. The scientific world, even while he was living, accounted him "the greatest chemical discoverer of his time." But in the early 'eighties, argon, helium, krypton were still undiscovered, and the brilliant years of scientific achievement and world recognition were still to come. The other day, when Lady Ramsay was with us, our united recollections carried us back, across those brilliant years, to a happy autumn holiday in the early 'eighties, to the little cottages in a Highland glen, and the little bridge over a peat-brown Highland burn.

One autumn after their marriage the Ramsays spent their holiday in Arran. We were there also, living in a white-harled cottage at the mouth of Glen Rosa; and they were farther up the Glen. It was a very happy autumn. Only once did any of us see the Professor what might be called professorially restive, and that was when a dear old friend of ours recommended to him her latest hobby—"decorticated bread." We were gathered about the wood-fire and the giant tea-kettle of a Highland picnic; the moors, with the rocks, the heather, and the bog-myrtle, were all around us. On one of the rocks they sat, a little apart from the rest of us, she talking with animation, he silently listening.

"I will explain the chemistry of it to you, Professor Ramsay," she said to him, "and then you will understand it. There are just five gases in the composition of the human body, and there are just five gases in the bread—the same gases!—and they go *straight* to feed the gases in the body."

Our two families shared many adventures, chief of which, I think, was a midnight climb to see the sunrise from the top of Goat Fell. One night, from our cottage door, we gazed on a silver fairyland. The moon had risen sheer over the pine-wood; the black headlands ran out into a silver sea; the low-lying deer-park, the burn winding below in the glen, were bathed in silver light; and far up in the summer sky stretched the mountain-side, so silver-clear that the very granite boulders glittered about the summit.

We set off about one o'clock in the morning along the moonlit road; the night warm and silent, the air sweet with honeysuckle, scarcely a leaf stirring. At a turn of the road a huge stag cleared the hedge at a bound; and farther on we surprised little groups of deer that flitted nimbly before us in the silver deer-park. At two o'clock we were in the pine-woods behind Brodick Castle, groping our way among ferns, fallen trees, and tall foxgloves; and then, in the moonlight again, the climb began, over a wide stretch of heather and bog-myrtle. At three o'clock, when the first halt was called, we were high up among the boulders. We had come very near to the moon. Far below us, now, lay the silver sea and the dark woods; the great grey boulders stretched above and all around us.

Then a change crept over the night. The moon waned: a cold steel-blue spread over the East. Somewhere there, Day was breaking.

We set out again silently, in single file, among the granite boulders. In another twenty minutes we should reach the top.

But where was the top? The peak we had seen sparkling in the moonlight had vanished —shrouded, in a cloud. A white mist came creeping down among the clefts and crannies of the rocks. We saw each other looming through it, contorted, visionary. Shut in by mists, the world for us shrunk into a few yards, we climbed now against an angry wind. On the long ridge we stepped warily; far below us, though we could not see it, dark Sannox lay, and the White Water, creeping like spilt milk in its rocky bed. Soaked in mists that were blown hither and

thither by the winds, we climbed the last
few yards almost on hands and knees.

Impossible to forget the splendour of the
vision from that grey, bitter-cold, wind-
swept mountain-top as we stood looking
down on the clouds whirling and racing
deliriously past our feet. Gradually they
resolved themselves in the East into one
dense wall of brown, red-rimmed cloud.
This, we knew, hid from us his solar majesty,
even now rising from his cold sea-bath.
Then the mists came down about us again,
swept before the gusts of the wind, and we
saw nothing. We had almost given up hope
when an involuntary cry of exultation rang
out. The wild mists had parted. For a
moment we saw the glorious molten Sun, a
flaming Sun, through seething mists that
met again and whirled headlong into space.
Breathless we stood and waited: and again—
and once again—it came. . . .

Everyone's memory includes a picture
gallery, constantly added to; landscapes—
seascapes—portraits; familiar faces, grave
and gay. These are some of the portraits
that have always hung on the line in my
portrait gallery. They are Victorians All.